don't you
    forget about me

don't you forget about me

Contemporary Writers on the Films of John Hughes

Edited by Jaime Clarke
Foreword by Ally Sheedy

SIMON SPOTLIGHT ENTERTAINMENT
New York | London | Toronto | Sydney

These works are memoirs. They reflect the authors' present recollections of their experiences over a period of years. Certain names and identifying characteristics have been changed and certain individuals are composites. Dialogue and events have been re-created from memory and in some cases have been compressed to convey the substance of what was said or what occurred.

SIMON SPOTLIGHT ENTERTAINMENT
An imprint of Simon & Schuster
1230 Avenue of the Americas, New York, New York 10020
Introduction and compilation copyright © 2007 by Jaime Clarke
Foreword copyright © 2007 by Ally Sheedy
John Hughes Goes Deep: The Unexpected Heaviosity of *Ferris Bueller's Day Off* copyright © 2007 by Steve Almond
A Slut or a Prude: *The Breakfast Club* as Feminist Primer copyright © 2007 by Julianna Baggott
Enchanted Night: The Magic of *Sixteen Candles* copyright © 2007 by Lisa Borders
On *Weird Science* copyright © 2007 by Ryan Boudinot
You Look Good Wearing My Future, or The Sexually Ambiguous Best Friend copyright © 2007 by T Cooper
Blowing It: My *Sixteen Candles* copyright © 2007 by Quinn Dalton
Can't Help Falling in Love copyright © 2007 by Emily Franklin
Pretty in Penury copyright © 2007 by Lisa Gabriele
That's Not a Name, That's a Major Appliance: How Andrew McCarthy Ruined My Life copyright © 2007 by Tod Goldberg
Which John Hughes Character Are You? copyright © 2007 by Nina de Gramont
La Vie en Rose: *Pretty in Pink* copyright © 2007 by Tara Ison
Ferris Bueller: An Infatuation, a Life Lesson, and One Harmless Family Adventure copyright © 2007 by Allison Lynn
Real Men Don't Eat Quiche: The Woes of Ferris Bueller and His North Side Buddies copyright © 2007 by John McNally
I Dated Molly Ringwald, Sort Of copyright © 2007 by Dan Pope
The Ghost of Ally Sheedy copyright © 2007 by Lewis Robinson
My Mary copyright © 2007 by Ben Schrank
The Scream, with Lip Gloss copyright © 2007 by Elizabeth Searle
Make a Wish: The First Kiss Lasts Forever copyright © 2007 by Mary Sullivan
In What Way Does the Author's Use of the Prison Symbolize . . . ?: A Deep Ego-Identification with Ferris Bueller copyright © 2007 by Rebecca Wolff
How John Hughes Altered My Life copyright © 2007 by Moon Unit Zappa
All rights reserved, including the right of reproduction in whole or in part in any form.
SIMON SPOTLIGHT ENTERTAINMENT and related logo are trademarks of Simon & Schuster, Inc.
Designed by Steve Kennedy
Manufactured in the United States of America
First Edition 10 9 8 7 6 5 4 3 2 1
Library of Congress Cataloging-in-Publication Data
Don't you forget about me : contemporary writers on the films of John Hughes / edited by Jaime Clarke ; foreword by Ally Sheedy.–1st ed.
p. cm.
ISBN-13: 978-1-4169-3444-8
ISBN-10: 1-4169-3444-8
1. Hughes, John, 1950–Criticism and interpretation. I. Clarke, Jaime, 1971–
PN1998.3.H84D66 2007
791.4302'33092–dc22
2006033122

To
Eric Tyrone McLeod
and
Aaron Quartullo
and
Sally Ullstrup
whose friendships have proved Hughesian

Contents

Acknowledgments

My heartfelt thanks go to the contributors of the fine pieces that make up this anthology. (Special thanks to Emily Franklin for all her help.) Too, I'd like to thank Ryan Fischer-Harbage for his steadfastness and for being the bridge to the equally passionate Terra Chalberg, editor extraordinaire. Thanks also to my wonderfully astute agent, Lauren Abramo, a perfect match a long time in the making. Finally, thanks to Mary Cotton, who graciously acted as research assistant for this anthology but who is so much more.

Foreword

John Hughes came into my life in 1984 and changed it forever. I don't believe that is an overstatement. He gave me the role of Allison Reynolds, which, I now see, was the role of a lifetime. *The Breakfast Club* has had such a long life, and who could have predicted that? It still isn't dated and seems to be approaching the status of a classic.

When I go to pick up my daughter from school, the high schoolers and middle schoolers come up to tell me how much they love the movie. I know that kind of attention used to bother Rebecca, but now, at twelve, she thinks it's pretty cool. And so do I.

John is a creative, open, appreciative, and honest director. He is the only writer-director with whom I have worked who is courageous enough to truly let his script go. He was never tied up or locked into chaining any actor to *exactly* what he wrote when it clearly didn't work. Or when there was a better choice. I think perhaps the only misstep we made was in changing Allison's appearance so drastically at the end. But even there he was open to a modification. I felt that Allison covered herself up to hide. The hair in the eyes, the white makeup and dark eyeliner. She looked fierce and hostile, which he loved. Underneath, of course, she was in great pain. I did not want her to apply even more makeup to change herself.

So what did he decide to do? First of all, he departed from his original idea of having her go through a traditional makeover. I wanted her to be uncovered, to emerge. Instead of having Molly Ringwald's character, Claire, paint her face, he decided Claire should be removing the harsh mask. I wanted the hair to come away from the face. Allison had been hiding behind it. Unfortunately, we ended up with a lace bow à la Madonna. Remember, this was the '80s. Also, we ended up with a pink, pretty top that was supposed to be an undergarment. Of course, in retrospect, I realize she would never have worn that. It should have been a sleeveless men's undershirt. But the point was Allison should have been transformed into a beautiful girl. I guess beautiful by a movie's definition. I think we probably should have left her alone or tried something a little less drastic and more original.

However, the fact remains that John changed the scene and the intent entirely. I cannot tell you how rare this is and how generous. The change came out of the way the movie was unfolding and especially the way the characters were developing. He trusted us. I felt trusted and appreciated. I felt seen and heard. Not just in this sequence, but through the whole filming. It gave me great courage and unlocked my imagination. I was never afraid to try new things or to go where Allison was taking me.

Another instance of this was in the pot-smoking scene. I didn't think Allison would risk the effects of marijuana. Especially the possibility of paranoia. She was *already* in that state. I didn't want her to suddenly open up her bag (and her mouth) to strangers because she was high. I thought it should be a conscious, brave decision. He *understood* me and agreed. He actually let me film an entire unscripted scene that involved a set change, rocking on a table, crying, and a Phil Ochs song just because, I guess, he liked the idea. Again, almost no one will do this. He wanted to see what would happen, how it would play out. The scene didn't make the final cut. He told me the powers that be thought it was too weird. But he gave me a real transition for her that carried her over a dangerous precipice in the story and took me on a ride through the rest of the movie.

I keep emphasizing trust because it is so unique and sort of brave in the process of making a film. John simply delegated other jobs to the talented people he had hired and spent his time working with us. Tom Del Ruth was our director of photography, and John would check the camera angle right before we shot and then go back to working with us. He never fussed about a setup, he never got involved in a technical argument. He wisely conferred mostly with Dede Allen, who was our brilliant editor and who worked in a room in the high school, editing as we went along. I never felt he needed to assert any kind of position of power.

One of my favorite memories of John is having him sitting right next to the camera while we filmed, watching and intensely enjoying everything going on. I don't remember him absent and watching by the monitor. It felt like we were all in it together. He really was the sixth member of the Breakfast Club.

I probably should end here, but I am sending out a long-overdue and very public thank-you letter here.

John, thank you for giving me the best role I ever had. Thank you for showing me what I was capable of. Thank you for watching, for trusting us, for so loving and appreciating every moment. You showed me what a great director can be and can do. I could never ever repay you. Thank you for giving me the experience of a lifetime.

Ally Sheedy

Introduction

If you're like me (and the evidence is inconclusive either way), you have a special place in your heart for the films of John Hughes. By virtue of holding this book, you probably knew a Ferris, a Duckie, a Samantha, or maybe even a Watts. Perhaps, too, your high school halls were filled with Hughes-speak. On any given day my classmates could be overheard aping the Hughes movies: someone yelling across the senior parking lot, "Only burners like you get high," or, "I'm off like a dirty shirt"; kids reassuring themselves by muttering, "We're safe as kittens"; someone shouting, "He pukes, you die," during a raucous drinking game; or "You're not dying. You just can't think of anything good to do" scrawled across the inside of a boy's-room stall. Then there was the year a particularly odious freshman arrived and departed every scene with the signature line from *Some Kind of Wonderful*: "I think it's safe to say that this party is about to become a historical fact." For those who came of age in the 1980s, the Hughes films deftly illuminated and assuaged the anxieties of an entire generation, as witnessed by the essays that follow.

Coming of age in the eighties, my friends and I loved the Hughes movies, and for the entirety of my sophomore year I believed I was Ferris Bueller. My job at the fish-and-chips down the street from my high school put me in a position of some power, as I insisted on feeding the popular kids and the school's security guards free of charge, a policy that bore fruit the time I was caught off campus (if I would've played by the rules, I'd have been in chemistry class), my then high school girlfriend wide-eyed with amazement as the security guard squired us to the far end of the football field to let us sneak back on campus as the bell rang; or the time I was caught sneaking onto another high school campus during lunch and was hauled in to see the principal, who threatened to call the police and have me arrested for trespassing. Ferris-inspired, I didn't for one moment believe that I wasn't capable of talking my way out of it.

As a role model, Ferris Bueller was a dangerous one: Once I learned that there were no wrong answers and that everything–I mean everything–was up for negotiation, my academic standing declined as my social standing ascended. I was that someone you should talk to, and I was only too happy to help, not just because I knew how to play the system to win, but because, like Ferris, I felt genuine affection for my classmates and treated everyone equally. (All of this was lost, of course, when I transferred to a rich private school where I was the poor kid who had to beat the after-school bell to get to his job at the fish-and-chips on the other side of town, but that's another John Hughes movie altogether.)

The anthology you're holding in your hands was put together in a bid at recapturing these salad days when, like the protagonists' in the Hughes movies, my thoughts were consumed with *Does she like me?* or *Why should I play by the rules?*–preoccupations that carried with them world-weighted consequences. There's no plainer way to say it. If you're like me (and by now let's just admit that you probably are, or could be), you can be minding your own business, going about your day–whatever it is you do–when a powerful wave of nostalgia crashes on your shores, triggered by something as innocuous as sitting in traffic next to the car you drove every day to high school, or a song on the radio you *loved*, much to the chagrin of your older, (probably) musically wiser self. And it's a powerful drug. If in my younger and more vulnerable days I was obsessed with Ferris Bueller, it's Iona from *Pretty in Pink* who lords over me now, admonishing me about the dangers of overdosing on nostalgia; and the more complicated life becomes, the more imminent the fear of flatlining.

As I began to solicit writers for this anthology, I wondered at the breadth of admiration for the Hughes films, a little worried that my not-so-private enthusiasm would be met with indifference. While I had no pretense that my own relationship with the Hughes movies was singular, it was always startling to encounter a complete stranger with whom I felt an instant, genealogical connection when the subject of the films arose. And so it was similarly startling when the essays collected here began to roll in by authors from dissimilar backgrounds and all geographic walks–each professing an acute obsession with or autodidactic insight into the Hughes films.

Part of the power of film is its ability to inspire a bond among filmgoers who may have nothing else in common. As the work in this anthology attests, the Hughes films meant a great deal to a great many and likely will for some time.

Jaime Clarke

John Hughes Goes Deep

THE UNEXPECTED HEAVIOSITY OF
FERRIS BUELLER'S DAY OFF

by Steve Almond

I missed *Ferris Bueller's Day Off* on the first pass, so I never quite understood what all the hubbub was about. And, as generally happens when I miss out on all the hubbub, I took it personally and thus bore a senseless grudge against the film, which I would routinely malign whenever people tried to explain how terrific it was. More often than not, I am really just a very big asshole.

Notwithstanding this, last winter I got sick, so sick I was reduced to raiding my landlord's DVD collection. He had about forty movies, most of which were thrillers of the sort that feature a European secret-agent babe who takes her shirt off and a picturesque decapitation. He also had *Ferris Bueller*.

I watched the film in a state of growing astonishment. It was, without a doubt, the most sophisticated teen film I had ever seen. I wasn't entirely sure it qualified as a teen film at all. It featured a number of techniques that I recognized from other, later films: direct addresses to the camera; on-screen graphics; the prominent use of background songs to create de facto music videos; the sudden, exhilarating blur of fantasy and reality.

More than this, though, John Hughes performed an astounding ontological feat. He lured viewers into embracing his film as an escapist farce, then hit them with a pitch-perfect exploration of teen angst. He sneaked genuine art past the multiplex censors.

I needn't belabor the basic plot—kid fakes being sick, outwits dopey grown-ups, gallivants around Chicago with pals. Hughes is, like any decent Aristotelian, more concerned with character.

Ferris himself (Matthew Broderick, unbearably young) comes across as a charming manipulator devoted to his own enjoyments. We initially encounter him playing sick on his bed. It is a stagy performance, and he seems mildly disappointed when his doting parents fall for it. We get a few scenes of him mugging for the camera and are introduced to his inept nemesis, the dean of students, Ed Rooney.

The scene shifts to a sleek, modern home, propped up on stilts and perched at the edge of a bluff. We cut to a dark, sarcophagal bedroom, littered with medicine bottles and crumpled Kleenex. A figure lies obscured under a blanket, like a mummy, while an electronic dirge plays in the background.

This is our introduction to Cameron Frye (Alan Ruck). The phone by the bed rings, and a hand appears and slowly clicks on the speakerphone. It is Ferris demanding that Cameron, his best friend, come over and spend the day with him. Meaning, essentially, chauffeur him around.

Cameron declines in a froggy voice. He is sick. Ferris repeats his demand and hangs up.

"I'm dying," Cameron whispers.

The phone rings again and Ferris mutters, "You're not dying. You just can't think of anything good to do."

We now see Cameron from above. His expression is one of resignation, giving way to despair. And then, fabulously, he begins to sing.

"'When Cameron was in Egypt's land . . .?'"

A rich, somber chorus of voices joins him: "'Let my Cameron go!'"

The invocation of the old spiritual is at once strange and revelatory. It has no business, really, in what has been—to this point—smarter-than-average teenybopper fare. But then, neither does Cameron Frye.

Hughes could have simply cast him as a straight man for Ferris. But he does something far more compelling: He renders the pair as a psychological dyad. Ferris is fearless, larger than life. He has internalized the unconditional love of his parents and skips through his days in a self-assured reverie. He is what every teenage guy dreams of being: a raging, narcissistic id who gets away with it. Cameron is an actual teenager: alienated from his parents, painfully insecure, angry, depressed.

It is the tension between these two that lies at the heart of the film and drives the action. Ferris dances around the house (accompanied by the theme from *I Dream of Jeannie*). Dad calls from work, and Ferris plays him like a Stradivarius. Then he turns to the camera and, with a look of indignation, says: "I'm so disappointed in Cameron. Twenty bucks says he's sitting in his car debating about whether or not he should go out."

Cut to Cameron at the wheel of a white junker, his long, rubbery face cast in a posture of despair. He sniffs. He stares ahead. He squinches up his eyes and growls, "He'll keep *calling* me. He'll keep calling me till I come over." He puts the key in the ignition, starts the car. He shakes his head and yanks the key out of the ignition. Then, with no warning, he starts to pound the passenger seat. These are vicious blows. "Goddamn it," he screams. The camera backs off to a midrange shot. We hear the car start again and the engine revs, and we hear a primal scream at the exact same pitch. Then the car goes dead. "Forget it," Cameron says. "That's it." He flings himself out of the car and stomps back to his empty house. We cut to a close-up of the empty driver's seat. Birds tweet. Suddenly we hear the crunch of his penny loafers on gravel and see a blurry image of Cameron's hockey jersey through the rear window. He is stomping back toward the car. We think: *Ah, he's given in.* Just then he stops and begins jumping up and down and throwing punches at some invisible adversary.

The sequence lasts barely a minute. It is an astonishing piece of physical humor, an emotional ballet worthy of Chaplin. Hell, it's one of the best pieces of acting I've ever seen, period. Because it's not just funny, it's heartbreaking. We are watching a kid crippled by his own conflicted impulses, torn between outrage and obedience.

In a very real sense he needs someone to take charge. Ferris is more than willing. Within a few minutes he has kidnapped Cameron, along with the prize Ferrari convertible Cameron's father keeps in the garage. Next he rescues his dishy girlfriend, Sloane, from school, and the trio tear off toward town.

Ruck is tall, blue eyed, big jawed, movie-star handsome. Broderick looks nebbishy by comparison. If the film had been made today, and by a lesser director, you can bet your Milk Duds that their roles would have been reversed. (Such are the mandates of the beauty gradient.) But Hughes clearly had a feel for his actors. And they so inhabit their roles that you wind up focused on their affect, not their cheekbones.

Hughes has long been hailed as the clown prince of teen angst. Whether it's Molly Ringwald getting felt up by her grandma (*Sixteen Candles*) or Ally Sheedy teasing her dandruff into a snowfall (*The Breakfast Club*), he knows how to put across the exquisite humiliation of adolescence. Still, most of his films play to formula. *Ferris Bueller* has its share. We know, for instance, that Ferris will prevail over Rooney in the end, and that he will make it home in time to fool his benighted parents.

But the film as a whole is a looser, more improvisatory affair. It has a dreamy, superannuated quality. There are all these odd, unexpected moments. A secretary pulls a pencil from her bouffant hairdo. Then a second. And a third. As a teacher drones on about the Hawley-Smoot Tariff Act, Hughes shows us a series of stark close-ups of students. These are actual teens—zits, bad hair, gaping mouths—and their expressions convey actual teen imprisonment: boredom, bewilderment, homicidal intent.

Even a character like Ed Rooney (played with transcendent unction by Jeffrey Jones) is granted his own impregnable sense of logic. He knows Ferris Bueller is making a mockery of his authority, and the educational mission, and that his popularity makes him the ideal target for a truancy jihad. "I did not achieve this position in life," he sneers, "by having some snot-nosed punk leave my cheese out in the wind."

There is no line in the universe that more succinctly conveys the Rooney gestalt.

Or consider what Hughes does with a visit by our heroes to the Art Institute of Chicago. He offers us lengthy shots, backed by a soft, symphonic score, of the most beautiful paintings in the world: Hoppers, Modiglianis, Pollocks. There is no ulterior plot motive; he is simply celebrating the majesty of the work. We see Cameron, Ferris, and Sloane stand before a trio of Picassos, transfixed.

As the music crescendos, we see Cameron standing before Georges Seurat's pointillist masterpiece, *Sunday Afternoon on the Island of La Grande Jatte*. We cut to a shot of Ferris and Sloane, the happy couple, necking in the blue light of a stained-glass window, then back to Cameron, alone, staring at the Seurat. Another one of those magical things happens: The camera begins zooming in on the little girl in white at the center of the canvas. We cut back to Cameron, closer now. Then back to the little girl. We see his growing anguish as he realizes that her mouth is wide open, that in fact she is wailing.

Okay, good enough: Cameron recognizes himself in the figure of this little girl whose mother is holding her hand but making no effort to comfort her. Got it.

But then Hughes takes us even deeper. He gives us an extreme close-up of Cameron's eyes, then cuts back to the canvas, to the girl's face, then to her mouth, then to the specks of paint that make up her mouth, until we can no longer resolve those specks into an image; they are just splotches of color on coarse fabric. This is the true nature of Cameron's struggle: His anxieties have obliterated his sense of identity.

This sequence gives way, somewhat abruptly, to a German street parade. Cameron is fretting. He needs to get his dad's Ferrari back to the house. Ferris objects. He wants to have more fun. But he also knows that his friend needs to loosen up, to conquer his fear and experience life.

The next time we see Cameron, he and Sloane are hurrying along the parade route. Ferris has ditched them. We cut to a float. Ferris has commandeered a microphone. "It's one of my personal favorites, and I'd like to dedicate it to a young man who doesn't think he's seen anything good today. Cameron Frye, this one's for you." He begins to lip-synch a campy version of "Danke Schoen." Then he launches into "Twist and Shout." The crowd goes nuts. Ferris has induced mass hysteria in downtown Chicago. This could never happen in real life. It is a Walter Mittyesque diversion. Which is precisely the point: Ferris has staged this adolescent fantasy of omnipotence expressly for his best friend.

• • •

By definition, the adults in a Hughes film are beyond hope of trans-formation. But it is his central and rescuing belief that teens are capable of change—even the ones who seem to be stock characters. I am thinking here of Jeanie Bueller (Jennifer Grey), who plays the overlooked younger sister and spends most of the film in a snit of sibling rivalry. She is so eager to bust her brother that she winds up in a police station, next to a spaced-out drug suspect (an excellent Charlie Sheen) who slowly chips away at her defenses to reveal the sweet, needy kid living beneath her bitterness.

The prime example, of course, is the relationship between Ferris and Cameron. It is without a doubt the most convincing therapeu-tic narrative in Hughes's oeuvre. After all, as much as we may want to suspend our disbelief, is there anyone out there who *really* believes that Molly Ringwald's character in *The Breakfast Club* is going to give Judd Nelson's the time of day once they're back in school?

Ferris himself is, for the most part, a fabulous cartoon—half James Bond, half Holden Caulfield. But he understands the very real crisis Cameron is facing and takes it as his role to push his friend into emotional danger.

But Ferris, of course, leads a charmed life. His existentialism comes cheap. For Cameron (as for the rest of us), the experience of pleasure is an ongoing battle against anxiety. Ferris and Sloane can treat the day as just another glorious idyll. For Cameron, it comes to assume the weight of a reckoning.

Toward dusk he, Ferris, and Sloane return to his house with the precious Ferrari intact. Ferris has a plan: They can run the accrued miles off the car's odometer by jacking the car's rear tires off the ground and running the car in reverse.

As they sit outside the garage, Cameron comes clean about his anxieties. "Being afraid, worrying about everything, wishing I was dead, all that shit. I'm tired of it." He looks at his friends. "It was the best day of my life," he says. "I'm gonna miss you guys next year."

The standard teen film would probably end on his upbeat note. Hughes is just getting started. Cameron heads into the garage to check on the car. Ferris's plan is not working. For a moment Cameron appears panic-stricken.

Ferris suggests they crack open the glass and adjust the odometer. But Cameron shakes his head.

"No," he says. "Forget it. Forget it. I gotta take a stand." His tone takes a sudden detour into self-loathing. "I'm bullshit. I put up with everything. My old man pushes me around. I never say anything." He is shouting now. "Well, he's not the problem. I'm the problem. I gotta take a stand. I gotta take a stand against him." As he leans over the hood of the Ferrari, his voice drops to a menacing register: "I am not going to sit on my ass as the events that affect me unfold to determine the course of my life. I gotta take a stand. I'm going to defend it, right or wrong."

He kicks the car. "I am so sick of his shit! . . . Who do you love? You love the car. You son of a bitch!" He continues to kick at the car: the rear bumper, the trunk, the taillights. These are not gentle little movie kicks. They are charged with a real violence of intent. Thanks to some clever crosscutting, we can see that Cameron has nearly knocked the car off its jack. He is close to tears; his entire body is tossed by the savagery. And thus it becomes clear what he's been afraid of all along: his own murderous rage.

"Shit," Cameron says, "I dented the shit out of it." He laughs in a manner throttled by regret. Ferris and Sloane—like the viewer—are watching this meltdown in a state of shock. After all, this is supposed to be just a funny little teen movie. But something has happened on the way to the happy ending: a much darker, more authentic psychological event. A catharsis.

"Good," Cameron says finally in a voice of forced assurance. "My father will come home, he'll see what I did. I can't hide this. . . . He'll have to deal with me. I don't care. I really don't. I'm just tired of being afraid. Hell with him. I can't wait to see the look on the bastard's face."

Cameron sets his foot on the beleaguered front fender, which, of course, sends the car tumbling off the jack. The rear wheels hit the ground with a skid, and the car crashes through a plate-glass window and off the bluff.

There is a long, gruesome moment of silence as the three kids try to grasp the magnitude of what's just happened.

"Whoa," Cameron says. "Holy shiiiit."

Ferris immediately insists on taking the blame. This doesn't feel particularly momentous, given the state Cameron is in. But it does mark a profound transformation in the Bueller weltanschauung. He has risen above his happy-go-lucky solipsism—probably for the first time in his life—and offered to sacrifice himself.

Cameron has undergone an even more radical change. He has developed what my students often refer to, admiringly, as sack.

"No," he says. "I'll take it. . . . I want it. If I didn't want it, I wouldn't have let you take out the car this morning. . . . No, I want it. I'm gonna take it. When Morris comes home, he and I will just have a little chat. It's cool. No, it's gonna be good, thanks anyway."

I hate trying to convey the power of this scene by setting down the dialogue alone, because Ruck is doing so much as an actor the whole time, with his body, his eyes, his voice. It will seem an audacious comparison, but I was reminded of those long, wrenching soliloquies at the end of *Long Day's Journey into Night.*

I have no idea who won the Oscar for Best Supporting Actor in 1986. It is painful—given the photographic evidence of my wardrobe—for me even to think about that grim era. But I can tell you that Alan Ruck deserved that statue. His performance is what elevates the film, allows it to assume the power of a modern parable.

Look: John Hughes made a lot of good movies. I've seen most of them and laughed in all the right spots and hoped for the right guy to the get the right girl, and vice versa, and for all the "troubled kids" to find "hope." I've given myself over to the pleasant surrender of melodrama. But Hughes made only one film I would consider true art, only one that reaches toward the ecstatic power of teendom and, at the same time, exposes the true, piercing woe of that age.

People will tell you they love *Ferris Bueller* because of all the clever lines, the gags. That's what people need to think. They don't want to come out of the closet as drama queens. It's not a kind age for drama queens. The world is too full of absent parents and children gone mean. But the real reason to keep returning to the film is because John Hughes loved those kids enough to lay them bare, and he transmitted that love to us.

Bless him.

A Slut or a Prude

THE BREAKFAST CLUB AS FEMINIST PRIMER

by Julianna Baggott

The history of eighties virginity can be broken into two eras–pre-*Breakfast Club* and post-*Breakfast Club*. Because that's when the truth was first spoken–the Prude/Slut Trap, the Double-Edged Sword of our Fragile Sexuality.

Let's imagine our eighties virginity in various forms (feel free to add bangles to any of the following images):

Form A: Virginity hidden up a sweater sleeve like a granny tissue–necessary, saved for an emergency, dainty, though embarrassingly old-fashioned

Form B: Virginity as a contractual agreement. It had loopholes, but the negotiation of those loopholes seemed heated and arduous and possibly binding in a court of law–or at least the court of public high school opinion.

Form C: Virginity as an enormous cardboard sweepstakes check–something reserved for a lucky winner, weighty, cumbersome, hard to carry around discreetly

Form D: Virginity as a protective rind padding the heart–if you'll allow me that much poetry

Form E: Virginity as a vulnerable flank

If asked, straight up, would you confess to virginity? Would you deny? Would you ask for a definition? Post-*Breakfast Club* the answer was clear: There was no good answer. Our culture was sick and we were caught in it–the catch-22, the inherent bind thrust upon us by our gender, our era. This was news to us then, the sickness of our culture. We girls felt a deep injustice, sure. We knew that hypocrisy was abundant and that we were supposed to be all things to all people. (Elasticity is the female's strongest Darwinistic trait– why we survive with such fitness and ferocity. Boys, poor boys. Who knew you'd be so undercut by the allowances handed over with the phrase "Boys will be boys." That's where things went wrong for you. Was anything ever expected of you after that? Really? You could be yourselves–and your repertoire shrank to burps and groping.)

But back to sex–or the lack thereof.

Here's the scene: I was waiting for my best friend, Kristin Rehberg, to get home from work. She was sixteen. I was fifteen. In other words, my life hadn't yet started and hers had. Kristin drove a mail truck–a retired one–though it still had tinny blue doors and the red light on top. No one, before or since, has driven a mail truck with more style. She had dyed her hair red à la Molly Ringwald. She worked at the Limited, and her boyfriend worked at the Gap. They could wave to each other from across the thoroughfare of the mall. I cannot explain how incredibly cool this was at the time. In any case: They saw all the mall movies before anyone else.

Now, keep in mind that a few times in your life someone–like John the Baptist–comes along, pulls you aside, and tells you that the world is about to change. Kristin whipped the mail truck up into the driveway, put it in park, climbed out, and said, "There's this new movie."

Kristin described *The Breakfast Club*–the group made up of five different types (a brain, an athlete, a basket case, a princess, and a criminal), the Saturday-detention setting, and some of the fallout.

But this was all setup for the astounding moment of pure revelation, which she did the best she could to recount.

Via the poufed lips of Molly Ringwald (Claire), and squinted at us through the black-eyelinered eyes of Ally Sheedy (Allison), John Hughes put it to us this simply:

ALLISON: It's kind of a double-edged sword, isn't it?

CLAIRE: A what?

ALLISON: Well, if you say you haven't . . . you're a prude. If you say you have . . . you're a slut! It's a trap. You want to but you can't. And when you do you wish you didn't, right?

There it was. We stood in her driveway, in the cold, speechless. What did this mean for us? How would we go on in light of this revelation? Someone had said the thing that we'd all known for a long time but hadn't had any words for. Someone had said it aloud: the truth.

I know that some of you—the ones I sometimes don't care for—are saying, "But this is archetypal. The Madonna/whore complex—it's been around forever!"

(a) Don't use the word "archetypal" here, please. I'm trying to write an essay about eighties virginity as seen by a Catholic girl drowning in eyeliner in Delaware. Save "archetypal" for your stiff, borderline-academic cocktail party banter.

(b) The archetypal Madonna/whore complex may have been part of the staple diet in certain circles of American culture—who knows where?—but it wasn't available to me and my stiffly hair-sprayed compadres at this point in time.

And (c) I know that you weren't always like this. I know that you went home after seeing *The Breakfast Club* and tried to apply

lipstick using your cleavage—or dreamed of seeing such a thing live—
and either way the word "archetypal" didn't cross your mind. And
God bless you for that!

I reacted to the Prude/Slut Trap in countless ways. It revved my
anger, and I was already plenty pissed off. You wouldn't have
looked at me and thought, *Now, there's an angry kid,* but I was. I
was sick of the battened-down existence of girlhood.

I started dating a kid with a Mohawk.

I started negotiating an affair with a cheerleader's boyfriend. We
whispered (sexy and bullying dialogue) among petri dishes and
wasteful little algebraic equations and the mini driver's-ed manuals.

When the kid with the Mohawk told me to never, ever go out with
the blond-headed kid on the wrestling team, I did so immediately.

And I couldn't even yet begin to decode this from the movie:

ANDREW: You're a tease and you know it. All girls are teases!

BENDER: She's only a tease if what she does gets you hot.

CLAIRE: I don't do anything!

ALLISON: *That's* why you're a tease.

Just because men are turned on, we've set something in
motion. They take our attractiveness personally—and because
they're pleased, they think we've done something purposely to
please them. We're culpable. We should finish what we start. This
kind of injustice was just an inkling of what lay in store for me as
a female. I wouldn't get to the full brunt of it for years. But I was
on my way.

The Prude/Slut Trap isn't the only truism in *The Breakfast Club.*

Here are a few others:

(a) Our teachers hated us. The principal makes $31,000 a year–according to Hughes's Vernon–and it isn't worth it. Sure, Vernon hates Bender–the criminal–but he hates all of the kids, actually.

It was my ethics teacher, Mrs. Watkins, who hated me the most. (Though my French teacher, Mrs. Surepont, was a close second. She was forever offering to "fix my wagon.") One day my ethics teacher explained that we were going to raise money to purchase large-screen TVs for elderly people who couldn't see well.

I asked if the money weren't more needed for inner-city kids who didn't have enough to eat.

She flipped. "You don't see me wearing Aigner shoes! You don't see me going on weeklong ski vacations!" The Aigners were on my best friend's feet. I had been guilty of the weeklong trip to Colorado two years before. "You don't know what it's like," she said, "to work at this high school summer, winter, spring, and fall and to want to buy this certain coat and not be able to buy it, and then to see a freshman, a *freshman*, walking down the hall in that exact coat!"

Vernon says of the criminal: "You want to see something funny? You go visit John Bender in five years. You'll see how goddamned funny he is!"

The truth is that some of our teachers, not all of them, but some, wanted us to fail out there in the real world. They had their own version of life, and we represented some pain in it. For my ethics teacher I represented wealth. I wanted to defend myself. I wanted to tell her that my father was raised by a single mother, in poverty, in West Virginia, his alcoholic father dead. I wanted to tell her that he made sacrifices and made his own way through engineering school and law school, and who was she to judge him for taking his family on a ski vacation? I was the spoiled kid. I was what was wrong with her world. My future failure would certainly have helped along her definition of justice–if her definition of justice hadn't already thoroughly eroded.

(b) The cruelty of *The Breakfast Club* is groundbreaking–it's light handed and disturbingly dark and realistic. The jock says to the criminal, "You don't even count. I mean, if you disappeared forever, it wouldn't make any difference. You may as well not even exist at this school."

And then, what's maybe even worse, because it isn't said in anger but just as simple fact:

BRIAN: So . . . so on Monday . . . what happens?
CLAIRE: Are we still friends, you mean? If we're friends now,
           that is?
BRIAN: Yeah.
CLAIRE: Do you want the truth?
BRIAN: Yeah, I want the truth.
CLAIRE: I don't think so.

And we all knew it was the truth.

When Bender shows us his cigar-shaped burn marks, when Andrew tells us he duct-taped some kid's butt cheeks together for his old man, when Brian tells us about his attempted suicide, it didn't come as a shock to us then. It came as a relief. There we were, not trussed up and artificially sweetened for TV sitcoms. That's what it was like–and more and worse. There was the story of that party where that girl passed out and was raped by someone with a pool stick. She didn't talk.

(c) And this:

ANDREW: My God, are we gonna be like our parents?
CLAIRE: Not me . . . ever.

ALLISON: It's unavoidable. It just happens.

CLAIRE: What happens?

ALLISON: When you grow up, your heart dies.

Thanks, Mr. Hughes.

A few days after I saw the movie, I was in the cafeteria with my people—a group of field hockey girls, a few with eating disorders. Some idiotic football players were spitting spitballs at some band geeks. But they weren't just football players and band geeks, not after *The Breakfast Club*. We were all trapped in the same ugly, dying organism: high school.

I walked over to the football players and said, "C'mon, knock it off."

One said, "Knock what off?"

"The spitballs. Just grow up a little."

"Don't I look grown up to you, little girl?" He had me by a hundred pounds and more than a half foot in height.

"Listen, asshole, just stop it with the spitballs."

"Oh, she's angry now!" He put his arm around me, rubbed my back. "Isn't she cute when she's angry?"

"Cute" was my trigger word—often true for short people. "Don't call me cute again."

"What's wrong, cutie? You're so cute!"

"I mean it, call me cute again and I swear it won't be pretty. . . ."

He paused and looked at me deeply in the eyes. "You're so cute."

I slapped him. He had a big head and a thick, rubbery cheek. He was fair, and the skin went red fast. Friends told me later that my small handprint was on his cheek for the rest of the day.

The long-term result was astonishing. All of the boys at that table seemed to fall in love with me and treated me with enormous respect. They addressed me politely in the halls. I'd feel someone watching me, and when I turned around, it would be one of them—all agaze.

It made no sense. It only encouraged me. To what? Refuse to accept a definition—a prude, a slut, a cutie. I knew that definitions wouldn't work for me, that I was volatile, unwieldy, and that was the only way I'd survive.

The Prude/Slut Trap is only a primer. That's the bad news.

As we age, traps are everywhere for women. In the workplace, if we're strong, we're a bitch. If we're soft, we're weak. Aging? We blame ourselves for our vanity and then for letting ourselves go. And motherhood? Don't get me started. It's a field of land mines. You only get to pick the way you want to be blown to smithereens.

At the end of the film Brian reads his essay in a voice-over. Part of it goes like this: "You see us as you want to see us; in the simplest terms, in the most convenient definitions."

The world is complicated. You'd think that, more than twenty years later, I'd want simple terms, convenient definitions. (Isn't that what politicians think we want?) I don't. I prefer the honest mess of life, the complicated truth.

My heart isn't dead yet.

Enchanted Night

THE MAGIC OF *SIXTEEN CANDLES*

by Lisa Borders

I have a confession to make. My twentieth reunion has come and gone, and I'm still obsessed with high school.

I should be over it by now, but to this day I'll read or watch almost anything about teenagers. Holden Caulfield and Jo March are as dear to my heart as Angela Chase and Lindsay Weir from the short-lived television series *My So-Called Life* and *Freaks and Geeks*. In a pinch I'll even watch the cheesy message movies about teens featured on the Lifetime network, the kind ABC used to show on its *After School Specials*—adolescents on drugs, having sex, listening to rock 'n' roll. What, I ask you, could give more visceral viewing pleasure?

But nothing scratches my teen itch quite like the films of John Hughes. Though his 1980s movies were billed as comedies, they portrayed teens with a degree of nuance and an understanding of their complex social strata that were largely missing from the films that had come before. He created a host of memorable characters and launched many a young actor's career; but of all the characters in Hughes's films, Molly Ringwald's portrayal of Samantha Baker in *Sixteen Candles* is the one I return to time and again. The film establishes Samantha as an everygirl who exists in a kind of social limbo, neither one of the cool kids nor a dork, neither beautiful nor unattractive. As one of the jocks puts it when her name comes up, "There's nothing there, man. It's not ugly, it's just . . . void."

Of course, Sam is hardly a void, and the jock's comment says more about him than it does about her. It also says a lot about the suburban high school they attend, its pecking order, and the various cruelties and humiliations that are part of most teenagers' everyday lives. We're all familiar with the stereotypes of extremes—the football captain, the prom queen, the geek, the computer nerd—and they populate *Sixteen Candles* just as they populate every high school campus. What we don't see often in film—in fact, what I believe may never have been shown in film before *Sixteen Candles*—are the kids caught in the middle, the Samantha Bakers who are cool enough not to want to be geeks, but not quite so cool that they can achieve it. Most of us were closer to that middle ground than we were to either of the extremes. I know I was.

As a novelist, I can cloak myself in excuses for being drawn to the teenage years. In high school we are at our most malleable; adolescents try on personalities like clothing, and as a result, the possibilities for a fiction writer are endless. As Ringwald's Samantha says to Anthony Michael Hall's the Geek, "A lot could happen over a year. I mean, you could come back next fall as a completely normal person," and that dialogue captures the essence of what draws me to the teen years repeatedly in my own writing. I'm fascinated with people who reinvent themselves, particularly with the magic of the transformative moment; and there is no single age group that transforms itself quite the way teenagers do.

The magic of transformation may be part of what causes me to revisit adolescence in my fiction, but there's something else that drives me back to this time in my own life: the feeling that I didn't quite get it right. I had a great time in college, especially my last two years, and an even better time in grad school, excepting the abject poverty. My twenties were a blur of indie rock bands, the cute boys who played in them, and my continual quest for the perfect margarita. I was a party girl during the latter part of that heady decade, the 1980s, and that was, in a sense, my transformation.

For I did not have a great time in high school.

It wasn't terrible, certainly not picked-on-every-day, spitball-bombarded, petrified-of-being-beaten-up-after-school terrible; that was junior high. By high school I'd worked hard to remove every tic, every idiosyncrasy, every scrap of individuality that I thought had led to my being tortured so mercilessly in seventh grade. In short, I erased my personality, or at least submerged it as deeply as I could. I was so insecure about my appearance that I remember wearing the previous year's tried-and-true clogs to the first day of tenth grade and bringing my brand-new Candie's to school in a bag, only slipping them on when I saw one of the popular girls wearing them. By junior year I was living in a complicated social limbo; through some rather ruthless social climbing I had become friendly with the popular girls without actually being popular myself. I had limp, fine hair that resisted my repeated attempts to fashion it into Farrah Fawcett–style curls; a mild to moderate case of acne; and an extra ten pounds that I could never shed, despite drinking copious quantities of Tab and occasionally subsisting on my "rabbit diet": lettuce leaves sprinkled with wine vinegar and a handful of grapes. I was not even close to being the ugliest girl in school, but I was equally far from being the prettiest. Occasionally a geeky or otherwise socially outcast boy would express interest in me, and I, in turn, would express mortification.

In short, I *was* Samantha Baker.

• • •

When she first appears on screen, Samantha is eyeing herself critically in the mirror, searching for a physical transformation that has not occurred. We learn that it's the morning of her sixteenth birthday, but, as she says to her best friend on the phone, "I look exactly the same as I have since summer. Utterly forgettable." As the day unfolds, we learn that Sam has a crush on Jake Ryan, the popular and gorgeous senior whose girlfriend is the prom queen, and that a freshman—the Geek—has a crush on Sam. By night's end the school's entire social strata will have turned upside down. Exchange student and überdork Long Duk Dong will prove himself to be a party animal; the Geek will wind up parked in a Rolls-Royce with the prom queen; and Jake Ryan will notice Samantha, pick her up at her sister's wedding, and belatedly celebrate her birthday, kissing her as a cake with candles blazes between them.

Sixteen Candles has been referred to as a fantasy, and over the years I've heard and read some grousing about the implausibility of it all. Boys like Jake Ryan never notice girls like Samantha Baker, these pessimists say, and they certainly don't dump their prom queen girlfriends for them. But it's only implausible if the viewer believes that all the recouplings in the film are permanent. I don't believe they are, and I don't think the film suggests it. The movie is about one enchanted night, a Friday evening when most of the movie's teenage characters get to shed their skins, to completely transform themselves. The magic of that night carries over to Saturday, where the film ends, but will it still shimmer in high school hallways in the harsh Monday-morning light? Most likely not, but that's hardly the point of the film. *Sixteen Candles* is about the moment when the impossible becomes possible, and there is nothing implausible about a moment like this happening to someone, anyone, over the course of four years of high school. It happened to me.

• • •

From the ages of six to thirteen I lived in the part of New Jersey popularized by Bruce Springsteen; and while my town was just slightly too far from New York City to be considered a suburb, it was Manhattan compared with the rural South Jersey city my family moved to when I started high school. My mom and I were used to having our pick of shopping malls within a few miles of our home, occasionally taking a short bus ride to the big Macy's in New York if all else failed. After the move we were stunned to find that the closest mall with the kind of department stores we liked was now forty-five minutes away, and that if we wanted a big-city store, we'd have to drive an additional forty minutes to the Wanamaker's in Center City, Philadelphia.

The first kids who were nice to me in my new high school expressed genuine shock that my mother and I had gone "all the way to Philadelphia" one Saturday to shop. One of these kids said that I "dressed like a Hot Shot," referring to a group of popular girls. She meant it as an insult, but I agreed, and decided then and there what my mission for the next four years of high school would be. I would become a Hot Shot.

The problem was that aside from my wardrobe, I had little in common with the Hot Shots. They were all either cheerleaders or very pretty, or both. My looks were resoundingly average, and I had always been possessed of the socially devastating combination of zero athletic ability and extremely good grades. Try as I might, becoming friends with these girls seemed impossible—until fate intervened. Sophomore year my family moved to a new house, down the street from two of the popular girls. And one of them was in several of my classes.

Thus I ditched the only kids who were willing to be nice to me when I first moved, the way a Hollywood mogul might ditch a starter wife, only to find myself existing on the periphery of the popular crowd rather than within it. The girl who was in my classes and I became good friends, and a couple of the others were nice to me, but the rest of the group never fully accepted me. Worst of all, the group's ringleader despised me.

She had bleached-blond hair, cornflower blue eyes, and a face set in a permanent sneer. She resembled nothing so much as a malevolent Barbie doll. Clearly dismayed that some of the others in her group had accepted someone like me, she began orchestrating as many events as she could that didn't include me.

"What could we do?" the other girls would say when I complained about this. "She didn't want us to invite you."

Even though there were times I did things with these other girls, times when Evil Barbie was busy with her boyfriend *de la nuit*, I spent more Friday and Saturday evenings than I would care to remember watching them all drive away from my friend's house down the street. And while they all had boyfriends, none of the boys I was interested in ever seemed to notice me. It wasn't a terrible high school life, as high school lives go; to anyone but the popular kids I *appeared* popular, and appearances seemed to really matter. Still, I was often lonely, and that's what made my enchanted night all the more amazing. For reasons that have never been clear to me, on this one Friday night in November when I was sixteen, I was invited along on an outing set up by none other than Evil Barbie, Her Peroxided Majesty.

The evening started at a restaurant on the South Jersey shore known for its haphazard enforcement of the drinking age, which was still eighteen. There was not an eighteen-year-old among the four of us, yet we managed to get served several rounds of strawberry daiquiris. I was self-conscious enough to look around and think that I had made it; here I was, drinking with three of the most popular girls in school, and two of them even liked me! All I needed to make the night perfect was for a cute guy to throw himself at me.

A few hours later it happened. After we left the restaurant, we went to a party thrown by friends of Evil Barbie's whose parents were out of town for the weekend. The hosts were boys; not only were they boys, they were *older* boys, boys a year or two out of high school. Of course, the fact that they were still living at home and inviting high school girls over to imbibe beer did not exactly bode well for their future prospects. And though I generally was a girl who thought a great deal about the future–I repeatedly envisioned my departure for college while listening to Bruce Springsteen's "Thunder Road," complete with the tattered graduation gown and the scorch marks I hoped to leave in the driveway–I was thinking only about the present that night. I had rarely dated, and what I really wanted, almost as much as I wanted to get out of that town, was for a cute boy to like me.

The weird thing was I *knew* something would happen that night. I could feel it earlier, driving to the shore on the way to that restaurant; there was magic in the air. And when we got to the party and it did happen–when this boy, two years out of high school and *really* cute, with the shaggy brown hair and long legs of speed skater Eric Heiden, engaged me in twenty minutes of meaningless conversation and then walked me off to a more private part of the house–I wasn't really surprised. It was as if I'd been sprinkled with fairy dust and, for that night, everything I desired would happen.

We did nothing much more than kiss, a fact that helps to preserve it in my memory as an enchanted evening. At sixteen I wanted to be kissed by a cute boy, but I didn't want it to go much beyond that–

yet another reason I wasn't truly popular. And the fact that I didn't let it go very far may be why, the following Monday in school, I was handed a note from a girl I didn't know well, a girl who tended to hang out only with older boys.

I think I actually burned the note one night in a fit of teen drama, but its text included, to the best of my memory, "I didn't mean to start something, I'm sorry. I have a girlfriend. I hope you find your special someone or something. Good luck."

It was the "good luck" that hurt the most, though the blow of the note was softened somewhat by the comma splice. I knew I couldn't really fall in love with a guy who didn't know where to put his commas. I turned the note over to several of my friends for handwriting analysis, and one was convinced that it hadn't been written by a guy at all; but the fact that he never called me after that night seemed to substantiate that he was, in fact, the author of the note.

At the time I thought I felt hurt by the rejection, but in retrospect, I wasn't, not really. I loved having something to analyze and turn over and over in my mind, strategies to discuss with my friends. I thrived for weeks on the melodrama of the note and filled pages with terrible adolescent poetry about it all. It also gave me an excuse to drive by the boy's house with my friends and attempt to peer through the windows without being seen, an activity that was far more exciting than listening to Joe Jackson or Elvis Costello in my bedroom by myself. Sure, I would have loved to have a boyfriend, but at least *something* had happened. I had been noticed by a cute boy, kissed by a cute boy. It made me feel older. It made me feel transformed.

I was in college when *Sixteen Candles* came out and going through a phase where the only films I would see were foreign or impossible to follow. As a result, I didn't see the movie for the first time until a few years after its release, which, as it turns out, was exactly the right time for me to see it. I was at the height of my party-girl phase, having the most fun I'd ever had in my life and occasionally wondering why I hadn't had more fun in high school. Wasn't that the time when most people had their fun? Conventional wisdom and most of the popular films of the day still seemed to say so.

Sensitive teenage girls who don't quite fit in with any of their school's cliques have become prominent in the filmic landscape over the past two decades, but it was John Hughes who started the trend. As I watched *Sixteen Candles* for the first time, it was a revelation to see a girl like me on the screen. Samantha isn't beautiful like her sister or the prom queen, but she's interesting and she gets herself noticed. Sam's own father even tells her in the film that he doesn't worry about her the way he worries about her sister, because "when you're given things kind of easily, you don't always appreciate them." I know it sounds corny, but it made me tear up the first time I saw *Sixteen Candles*, for I was already starting to realize how true it was. I loved the life I was living by then, but from friends who'd gone to our five-year high school reunion, I'd heard that Evil Barbie's life didn't appear to be going as well. I don't know if this was true, but I believed it at the time. *Sixteen Candles* suggested that the Samantha Bakers of the world would lead more interesting lives than the prom queens, and the message not only felt prophetic to me, it also led me to an unexpected sympathy for the girl I've been calling Evil Barbie. She wasn't really evil. Sure, she'd been bitchy toward me, but she hadn't done anything to deserve a tough adult life while she was still so young.

It's this broader message *Sixteen Candles* suggests about life beyond high school that makes me feel it wouldn't matter if Jake Ryan got back together with the prom queen at school the following Monday, even if he passed Samantha a note similar to the one I got when I was sixteen. Sam had had her enchanted night, her night when the constellations aligned and everything she had innocently wished for came true. She was transformed. I've seen *Sixteen Candles* more times than I can count, and I've never cared much about what happened to Jake or the prom queen after high school. But I've always known that Sam would continue to metamorphose, and at some point—maybe in her twenties, maybe sooner or later— she would be seen by others as the person she wanted to be.

I know it, because it happened to me.

On *Weird Science*

by Ryan Boudinot

I watched *Weird Science* in a hot and smelly theater when it was released in the summer of 1985. A fluffy piece of matinee bait, it's a departure from the puppy-love, prom-worshiping, basically realist comedies in John Hughes's string of teenage fantasias. I appreciated the movie's science fiction flourishes and the introduction into my vocabulary of the term "air biscuit." I was, in other words, the movie's target demo.

That was the summer I attended Young Authors Camp, a week-long gathering of grade-school kids at Fort Casey, an old military installation on Whidbey Island in Washington State. Set on a bluff overlooking Puget Sound, with cavernous bunkers, a beach, and decommissioned cannons pointed to sea for a Japanese invasion that never arrived, the place was a paradise to me. While the soccer camp kids had to rough it in the barracks, the Young Authors campers spent the week in the officers' mansions, gathering around parlor fireplaces, where we'd discuss haiku and Native American folktales. It was like Yaddo for writers who occasionally cried because they missed their moms. Each of us young authors had begun to gravitate to particular genres and areas of specialty. There was a boy who had conducted lengthy correspondences with comic-book writers and grilled them about the finer details of their craft. Another kid wrote a series of poems about his roommate's stinky feet. Then there was Daniel, who was writing the novelization of *Weird Science*.

I thought this was brilliant. We had all been looking for an angle to get published since Rusty Miller, at age fourteen, made national news for selling his *Star Wars* trivia book. Miller had made enough money from the *Jedi Master's Quizbook* to completely pay for college, had appeared on *That's Incredible!*, and had stoked in us young writers an intense competitive streak. (The first time I met the editor of this anthology, we got to drunkenly talking about the writing projects of our '80s childhoods. I asked him if he remembered Rusty Miller. His response: "Rusty Miller! I wanted to *kill* that motherfucker!") A novelization sounded like a can't-miss proposition.

Daniel's plan to novelize *Weird Science* involved a twenty-page draft of the opening scenes and a series of letters to John Hughes and others involved in the film's production describing the market's need for such a work of literature. We were bewildered as to why these letters had not elicited a response from the filmmakers. How could they not see the need for a novel of this superb film? Episodes of *Doctor Who* were novelized, why not *Weird Science*? We pondered these questions while waiting for the lunch bell to ring. Maybe Daniel needed an agent, I suggested. Or maybe he should stick with knockoffs of Kwakiutl folktales.

Weird Science is a masturbation fantasy for boys who haven't yet figured out how to masturbate. From the first scene we're asked to root for Gary and Wyatt, the archetypal geeks who can't get laid, played by Anthony Michael Hall and Ilan Mitchell-Smith. It's hard not to feel sorry for them, pantsed as they are by Robert Downey Jr. in front of a gymnasium full of girls. From here the movie lays down a pleasing story arc of cojones acquisition, represented as much by Gary and Wyatt's increasing popularity among their peers as by fulfillment of their sexual urges. Here's how they solve their problem: They hack into a military computer, experience some bitchin' graphics, scan a photograph of Albert Einstein, and wear bras on their heads. After a lightning storm and fake fog worthy of a Ratt video, their dream woman appears in a doorway, ready to guide them down the path of sexual conquest and maturity. In 1985 dream women wore half shirts and spoke with British accents; thongs were things you wore on your feet at the beach. Yet *Weird Science* is kind of timelessly relevant to those encumbered with a Y chromosome, a realization of every conversation between male, acne-ravaged virgins in which the words "Yeah, I'd fuck her" are uttered.

The star of *Weird Science* is Hall, John Hughes's frequent muse, an actor whose mild speech impediment, awkward, lanky frame, and cylindrical head coifed with poofy blond curls invited both derision and identification. In every Hughes film Hall walked through he became a locus for audience sympathies. Yeah, you wouldn't be caught talking to him in the library, but he made you laugh and was a visual reminder for universal teenage awkwardness. Secretly you knew the guy was the ugly duckling destined to become a cool dude, which has basically been the trajectory of Hall's roles. One director called the collaboration between Hughes and Hall "the most promising since James Stewart and Frank Capra." That was Stanley Kubrick talking. In fact, Kubrick had him in mind when looking for the lead for *Full Metal Jacket.* Hall walked off the set of that masterpiece when he got fed up with the moody auteur's demanding directorial methods. Our loss, Matthew Modine's gain. Hall nonetheless paid the legendary director a compliment by saying, "Off camera, he's very quiet. He'd often be walking around quietly, twirling his hair while thinking about his next shot. I think the guy's a genius. I think the guy's a social hypnotist. I think he's incredible. He's onto something big-time. . . . If this doesn't make $100 million, something's wrong. I smell a sequel."

Actually, sorry, no, that's Hall talking about Tom Green on the set of *Freddy Got Fingered.*

Anthony Michael Hall went on to portray Bill Gates to Noah Wyle's Steve Jobs in *Pirates of Silicon Valley*, a solid 1999 made-for-TV movie about the PC and operating system revolution of the 1980s. The casting of Hall in *Pirates* introduced a layer of knowingness to what could have been a throwaway dramatization of Chairman Bill's rise; by placing the representative übernerd of the '80s in the role of the *actual* übernerd of the '80s, *Pirates* cast a backward glance at those Hughes movies in which the actor was a magnet for our amusement. In *Pirates* we're asked to laugh not at the expense of Hall as Gates, but at the brass at IBM, Xerox, and the investment community who failed to grasp the magnitude of his revolutionary ideas. Wyle's Steve Jobs stumbling out of a bank with his prototype Mac after being denied a business loan is humiliation in the same neighborhood with Gary finding his shorts around his ankles in front of the girls' gymnastics team. In both instances the audience sympathizes with these ostensible losers and invests in what will most certainly be their triumphant revenge. In both cases revenge comes out of a computer.

Weird Science and *Pirates of Silicon Valley* are two versions of the same movie, both tales about obtaining power through technology, and the unforeseen consequences of such power. In one movie the principals go for a joyride in heavy construction equipment; in the other they do the same in a convertible. In *Pirates*, Bill Gates looks surprised to see a motorcycle in the lobby of Apple Computer's corporate headquarters. In *Weird Science* a mutant biker gang disrupts a house party by crashing through windows and peeling out on the hardwood. See? Same flick. Let's move on.

For Bill Gates and Steve Jobs what computers wrought were

operating systems, applications, and unfathomable riches. What comes out of a computer for poor, unfuckable Gary and Wyatt is Kelly LeBrock, the model-turned-actress who, in a cosmetics commercial, lent the Reagan era one of its most representative phrases, "Don't hate me because I'm beautiful." She now appears on *Celebrity Fit Club*, trying to convince people not to hate her because she's "fat."

LeBrock also starred as the title character in *The Woman in Red*, which I assumed, incorrectly, was the source of one of the most cloying ballads of the 1980s, Chris de Burgh's "Lady in Red." Compare this with the insanely catchy, eponymous *Weird Science* theme song, performed by Oingo Boingo, led by Danny Elfman, who would soon ditch pop stardom to work in movie sound tracks for the likes of Tim Burton. It's a shaky, blippy piece of work, an argument for all that was fun about '80s music. Punchy horns and frantic computer squirts, a reverb-laden drum track and a nod toward *Bride of Frankenstein* in the form of a sample ("She's alive!") lead to Elfman's inventory of the supernatural: "Magic and technology / Voodoo dolls and chants." The frenetic verses bump right into the guitar anthem choruses, trading in jerky techno rhythms for confident riffs. It's almost as though Gary and Wyatt's transformation from nerds to studs is enacted in the music itself, sort of a rare feat of meaning for a sound track. "Weird Science" the song is so great that Hughes plugged it into the movie three times, at the opening and closing credits, and during the sequence when supernatural forces suck the clothes off a girl inexplicably playing piano at a house party.

Alongside the nerd-stud axis there's a technological-supernatural axis at work in this seminal Hughes film. To create his dream woman, Wyatt uses a Memotech MTX512 with an FDX add-on, a pre-DOS system introduced in 1983. This computer was manufactured in

Britain, the same place that manufactured Kelly LeBrock. According to one magazine ad, "the MTX ROM has been designed to allow maximum interaction between components of the software. A single program can be written which uses NODDY to display text and graphics, and a BASIC control program which calls routines written in assembly code. This is a feature of future generation computers not available on any other micro." In another ad the keyboard for the MTX512 is pictured next to an airbrushed graphic of a Porsche. One adjective alone can describe this advertising strategy: boss. The ads fail to mention that the MTX512 could be used to generate lightning storms and create a nuclear warhead from the cover of *Time* magazine. They also seem oblivious to the fact that a little company from Redmond, Washington, was about to thoroughly rock their world, much like a computer-generated woman with hair the size of a beach ball shopping for underwear made of barbed wire.

Weird Science anticipated geek sexuality, in which computers are a necessary intermediary step to sexual gratification. In lieu of actual interpersonal skills Gary and Wyatt use their left-brain computer hacking skills to create a "girl" who guides them to self-confidence, the key to gettin' the ladies. The process of building a white boy's self-confidence apparently begins by patronizing blues bars in African-American neighborhoods and getting drunk enough to lapse into Ebonics monologues. The movie ends not with Gary and Wyatt in a torrid three-way with LeBrock's Lisa (named, incidentally, after the first Apple computer with a GUI), but with them wooing two popular girls who previously dated the guys who humiliated them at the start of the movie (Robert Downey Jr. and Robert Rusler). The movie can be read as an argument for tenderness and a repudiation of overt machismo; the comeuppance of Wyatt's older brother, Chet (Bill Paxton), in which he's transformed from a militaristic, gun-wielding dickhead into a flatulent, animatronic Jabba the Hutt knockoff is one of the movie's funnier and most gratifying gags. Paxton adds an element of oedipal struggle to the story, with his flattop, grotesque facial contortions, and camouflage standing out as symbols of the extreme masculinity the movie seeks to subvert. In opposition to the radiant, enlightening sun that is Paxton's performance, LeBrock's Lisa is sorta motherly.

But *Weird Science* wouldn't feel as winning if Gary and Wyatt simply got laid. If LeBrock rocked the cradle of love with these two suburban boys whose parents are conveniently out of the picture, we'd have on our hands a prostitution fable like *Risky Business*. Or to put it another way, the fact that LeBrock doesn't fuck the boys allows this movie to blossom into a romance. It's telling that in the very first scene Gary's expressed fantasy doesn't revolve around sex so much as it gravitates to the romantic prelude of getting to know a girl. And although Wyatt is treated to a make-out session with Lisa, he passes out when the opportunity arises to go all the way, and wakes the next morning to find himself wearing her panties. Just as Hall's character in *Sixteen Candles* bartered for Molly Ringwald's panties, which he presented to his fellow nerds as proof of a conquest that never happened, Wyatt's acquisition of Lisa's totemic undies accomplishes the same thing, proving his character's virility without actually having performed any act that would have pushed this teen comedy into R-rated territory.

Speaking of romance, according to the Internet Movie Database, Ilan Mitchell-Smith, the actor who played Wyatt, left acting for good in the early nineties to pursue an academic career in medieval studies. He recently received his PhD from Texas A&M, where he completed his dissertation, "Between Mars and Venus: Balance and Excess in the Chivalry of the Late-Medieval English Romance," and previously studied at Fordham University and

UC–Davis. We've come to expect child actors to provide a lurid and morbid element of celebrity worship, so Mitchell-Smith's postacting achievements may initially strike us as freakish—shouldn't this guy be doing meth with minors in the exurbs of Las Vegas? But no, he belongs to a rarified clique of former child stars who have gone on to success in other arenas, like Danica McKellar, the actress who played Winnie in *The Wonder Years*, who became a mathematician of some renown at UCLA. (The Chayes-McKellar-Winn theorem? That was her.). Mitchell-Smith said screw it to acting after appearing in the early-nineties trash TV show *Silk Stalkings* as a rapist. He turned to academic life, and from all outward appearances, it suits him.

In a 2002 interview with the *Austin Chronicle*, Mitchell-Smith displayed some humor and perspective about his previous life as "the other one" from *Weird Science*. He still gets asked about his experience starring in the Hughes classic: "A standard question is 'What was it like to kiss Kelly LeBrock?' The truth is, that it's weird to be 15 and kissing a woman who is 30, who wouldn't be kissing you unless she had to. It's weird in all kinds of ways and not really that great. But that's not the answer the guys want. Because no matter what I say, the next thing he says is, 'Dude, I would have *fucked* her.' You're 15. She's married to Steven Seagal. How are you going to bring that about?"

I attempted to make contact with Mitchell-Smith to ask about his post–*Weird Science* career in chivalry and jousting, but repeated e-mails went unanswered. I wanted to see if there was a thread, however tenuous, between the man who wrote "Between Mars and Venus" and the kid who walked around in Kelly LeBrock's underwear. I enlisted the help of my brother, David, a librarian and archivist, who has access to some mystical librarian databases yet was unable to unearth copies of Mitchell-Smith's master's thesis or doctoral dissertation. I called the library at Fordham to request a copy of the thesis and was told they didn't have one. I got the same answer when seeking Mitchell-Smith's dissertation at Texas A&M. When I started to feel like a celebrity stalker, I called it quits. So with nothing to go on but the title of his dissertation, I concluded that Dr. Mitchell-Smith, he who once floated an air biscuit, had considered the gender divide represented in John Gray's pop-psych bestseller *Men Are from Mars, Women Are from Venus*, applied it retroactively to medieval romance lit, and found the state of male-female relations both balanced and excessive. If only I had a Memotech MTX512 with an FDX add-on.

Three days before the deadline for this essay I finally received a reply from Dr. Mitchell-Smith. He apologized for not getting back to me sooner and told me his dissertation is being published by a small press, with the original document placed in something called a "copyright hold." Hence my difficulty finding "Between Mars and Venus" via an academic route. However, he was kind enough to provide the abstract for the book, which outlines a five-chapter work considering the chivalric masculine identity in late-medeival romances. Dr. Mitchell-Smith argues that rather than considering the works of this period as representing conflicts between masculine and feminine identities, we can read these texts as expressions of the balance between two extremes of masculine behavior—courtly amorousness on one end and knightly violence on the other. These impulses were based on extreme ends of a cosmological model that was gaining literary currency at the time:

When Chaucer extols the reader to go "Forth, pilgrim, forth! Forth beste out of thy stal!" in his poem "Truth," he is equating the religious journey of the soul with a rejection of the temporal urges that humans share with animals. The differentiation between the rational soul (which is always seeking upwards towards God) and the temporal body (which is always driven towards the excesses of animal behavior) is an element of university-based cosmology that was becoming common in vernacular writers such as Chaucer and Gower.

My guess that the title for Dr. Mitchell-Smith's dissertation was a reference to a pop-psych bestseller was wildly off base and uninformed. Rather, the Mars-Venus axis refers to Geoffrey Chaucer, who "redefines the poles of excessive behavior in terms of astrological inclination, so that the worship and subservience to the gods Mars and Venus (by Arcite and Palamon, respectively) is simultaneously understood by the reader as excessively *marcien* and *venerien* planetary influence."

While chapter one of "Between Mars and Venus" "interprets chivalry as a preferred form of masculine activity along a spectrum of male behavior," the second chapter considers the tournament as an arena for changing masculine identity between the twelfth and fifteenth centuries. It was in this circumscribed performance space, Mitchell-Smith posits, that masculine expression evolved from group-oriented displays of combat to "individual spectacles of self definition that balance martial feats with courtly displays." Later chapters isolate Chrétien de Troyes' *Erec et Enide* and Chaucer's "The Knight's Tale" as further illustrations of Mitchell-Smith's model of chivalric excess.

Mitchell-Smith tells me the book is coming out in the next two years from Lexington Books, an imprint of Rowman and Littlefield. I'm totally going to buy it. I find it fantastically cool that the same person who wrote, "Chaucer makes a departure from the romances of the previous chapters and places the model of balanced chivalry within a Boethian framework, connecting planetary influence with an over-reliance on the urges of the temporal world," also once said, "You know Gary, for the first time in my life I don't feel like a total dick."

What strikes me as most fascinating, though, is how we might consider *Weird Science* under the same microscope Dr. Mitchell-Smith uses to view Chrétien. If we accept this model of masculine extremes—overly violent on one end and overly amorous on the other—Gary and Wyatt appear to fall into the middle. They're not as masculine as shotgun-wielding mutant bikers, but they're not so gentlemanly as to be above creating a woman from scratch for their own devices. It would seem that Wyatt/Dr. Mitchell-Smith presents us with a cognitive Möbius strip, enacting in one phase of his life a fairy tale about masculinity, while in another phase contributing to our understanding of the medieval origins of such narratives. Perhaps one reason why *Weird Science* was so appealing in 1985 and remains noteworthy today is that the questions it poses about how to become a man have been with us a long time. When we watch *Weird Science*, we're witnessing mythology with an Oingo Boingo sound track. One might find this argument a stretch, but it's my creation.

You Look Good Wearing My Future, or The Sexually Ambiguous Best Friend

by T Cooper

Teenagers aren't inherently interesting. Anybody who has ever been one knows this, and that's precisely why ex-teenagers of a certain age love us our John Hughes films: He makes teens look smart, stylish, smooth, witty, mature, and utterly fascinating. But more important, he makes it seem as though the concerns of teenagers are as crucial and weighty as those of adults, and that teenagers have some measure of control over their miserable lives—a complete myth on both counts. And yet we looked to Hughes films to see ourselves, or at least versions of ourselves to which we aspired. Some of us even went so far as to emulate specific aspects of Hughes's films in our daily lives, in hopes of causing a little bit of that veneer of significance to rub off on our decidedly more quotidian realities. I myself, inspired by *Sixteen Candles*, embarked upon more than a couple panty raids in bedrooms belonging to various older girls at my high school. One time I even partook in a behind-the-library, *Breakfast Club*–like smoke-out with my high school's resident Judd Nelsonesque burner.[1] And I'm not ashamed to admit that I borrowed Ferris Bueller's palm-licking and forehead-wetting techniques to convince my parents that I was too sick to attend school on a few occasions.

---

1. Well, maybe it was more than that one time.

My most overt cribbing from Hughes's films, however, was of the fashion variety. I'm comfortable enough with my overall fashion forwardness these days to admit that I did try, for at least a semester of high school, to wear leather half-gloves like Mary Stuart Masterson in *Some Kind of Wonderful* and Judd Nelson in *The Breakfast Club*. It was to be my trademark look, but unfortunately, it appeared terribly incongruent on days when I didn't have to wear my volleyball or soccer jersey (worn only on game days to advertise after-school matches). Further inspired by *SKOW*, I owned at least four blue chambray button-down shirts, which were in constant rotation in my wardrobe (Eric Stolz's character, Keith, wears a blue chambray shirt in all but a couple scenes). I didn't realize you need ridiculously light eyes and red or strawberry blond hair (neither of which I have) to look really good in these shirts, but nevertheless, for two straight years it was my uniform (with a short-lived, more preppified resurgence in college).[2]

Sometimes I'd roll up the sleeves, sometimes rock them with jeans, sometimes with surf shorts—I even cut off the arms of one of these prized shirts and wore the thing frayed and sleeveless on warm days, tucked into pleated khaki shorts with a braided light brown leather belt. My best friend called me a Snausage once when I dressed like that, and it still haunts me anytime I'm inclined to tuck in a shirt. What else? Of course: wrestling shoes and vintage bowling shirts like Duckie in *Pretty in Pink*; making a soap Mohawk and rocking out to a waterproof radio while in the shower (Ferris); and huge diamond (well, cubic zirconia) stud earrings (central symbols of both transclass and transgender understanding in *SKOW* and *The Breakfast Club*).

---

2. I wore these shirts so frequently that when it came time for college counseling at the end of eleventh grade, my assigned counselor, Mrs. Balak, suggested—I swear I'm not making this up—that I consider East Coast colleges because of my wardrobe: "You already dress the part," she said. I did indeed end up at a liberal arts college in Vermont where everybody was, in fact, wearing chambray button-down shirts from J. Crew. So I guess I'm left to consider whether *SKOW* is solely responsible for this momentous decision in my life, as I haven't been back to the West Coast to live since I was seventeen.

But the most egregious and deliberate example of my directly adapting fashion from film was via *Ferris Bueller's Day Off*. The minute I spotted it in that dark theater, I fell in love with Ferris's trademark crazy animal-print vest. Or modified animal-print/art-pattern vest. Whoever was on wardrobe should've been given a promotion for that one.[3] I loved that vest so much that when there was a homecoming dance coming up early during my senior year, I went out in search of one exactly like it. I combed both new and vintage stores across the Los Angeles area, from Melrose to Venice, the Beverly Center to Westwood, and on over to Santa Monica Place.[4] After a good week of hunting, find it I did—new, from Bullocks. This vest was more blue hued than Ferris's, but still, it was the same idea, and it was awesome, and even though I bought it a week before the dance, I didn't wear it to school because I wanted to debut it on the night of the actual dance.

Here I am in a yearbook photo snapped that night, beside Lori S——, one of my friends at the time:

© Alison Whitman Davidow

---

3. Ah, the wonders of the World Wide Web: I just checked the Internet Movie Database (imdb.com) and found that Marilyn Vance was responsible for costume design on this film; so big ups to Marilyn. And if it was one of Marilyn's overworked—and overlooked—wardrobe assistants who found and selected Ferris's vest, then my apologies, and those big ups are for you. (I also noticed that Dennis Grisco is listed as "dog supplier" for the film, so I want to send a big shout-out to him, too, because that rottweiler protecting the Bueller home from Principal Rooney was truly terrifying.)

4. Coincidentally located across the street from Trax record shop, where Andie worked in *Pretty in Pink*.

Yes, that's me on the right in my Ferris Bueller vest (if you can make it out through all of the layered, feathered hair). As you can see, I eschewed my *SKOW*-inspired chambray shirt for the night, deciding to pair my new vest with a white, Nehru-collared, long-sleeved shirt instead. Of course I considered a white short-sleeved T-shirt like Ferris's, but it was, after all, a dance, and I felt the need to dress up somewhat; short sleeves under the vest, I'd decided, would be for daytime use, regular school hours, during which I intended to roll out my vest at least twice a week. It, like the leather fingerless gloves, was also to be a trademark look. Oh, and here's the caption, to complete the picture:

> Seniors T——[5]Cooper and Lori S—— get down to Young MC's "Bust a Move" at the Homecoming dance.

I'm not entirely certain you can deem the activity depicted in that photo "getting down". . . and as I look at it now, for the first time in a long time, I'm thinking a more pressing issue suggested by the photo might be: "Were you queer in high school?"

Ah, no. Well, yes. Um, sort of. Wasn't *everybody*?

In retrospect, I guess the platonic dance reproduced above could be considered "queer." But only in retrospect. At the time: no, never. Girls danced together all the time, didn't they? And that was Lori S——, literally one of the most popular (and straight) girls in the school. And at the time I even had a boyfriend, Jason M——, and I'm sure Lori had a boyfriend too. I think it was the handsome star running back of the football team, who had graduated the year before—so no, there is nothing "queer" at all about the photograph.[6]

---

5. Yes, I did have a full first name that was once used in yearbooks and class rolls and driver's licenses, etc. But everyone—including my family—always just called me "T," and this is my story so I'll be damned if I have to include my full name here.

6. Come to think of it, I have no idea where my "boyfriend" would have been at the time this photo was taken, or whether I even attended the dance with him (I assume I would've); my only memory of the night is thanks to the existence of this photo and things related to it (like the vest).

But back to my vest. I rocked it, right? *I* thought so. But only until I came across some underclassmen later that night, coincidentally also captured in a photo in the yearbook, appearing just above the photo in which Lori S—— and I "get down to Young MC" on the dance floor:

© Alison Whitman Davidow

Freshmen Marcy D—— [left] and Austen M—— rest outside the gym. After dancing the whole night, tired students went outside to be refreshed by the evening air.

Set aside for a moment the astounding fact that this hard-hitting homecoming coverage, including evocative captions like the one above, won our yearbook a big prize that year. Can you see what she's wearing, there on the right?

THE SAME FUCKING VEST I WAS WEARING!

I was a senior! She, a lousy freshman! And it's a GUY'S VEST! What gall! A freshman? I didn't even know her name, and there she was, wearing the vest like you were *really* supposed to wear it–like Ferris wore it: over a simple white T-shirt with rolled-up sleeves–none of this arty Nehru business I was attempting. Her mother probably bought it for her, for chrissake, because there was no way a freshman was going to get to Bullocks by herself to pick out and buy a new vest for the homecoming dance. So basically, I had the same taste as Austen M——'s

Bullocks-loving mother, and as if it weren't terrible enough that I had to be seen in the same mom-approved vest as a freshman that night, the both of us had to be immortalized in our yearbook for all of eternity.[7]

Pulling out high school yearbook photos? See, I told you it gets boring when people start nattering on about themselves as teenagers. But the reason I just did is because there is clearly some other "dancing around the issues"[8] going on here: What I think I saw of myself *most* in Hughes's films was not something external, like clothing and those wacky, yet typically high school scenes I saw echoed in my life (though it was of course easier to focus on the outside than anywhere else). No, to be perfectly honest, what I latched on to in these films were the ways in which differences in gender and sexuality were portrayed within the context of various "everyday" high school settings. As is usually the case where teenagers are involved, it is always fair game to pick on differences in sex and gender, and I kept close tabs on the occasions on which Hughes's films reflected the easy joke:

- "Open this Locker and you Die! FAG!" scrawled across a locker in *The Breakfast Club*. That particular phrase may not have been scribbled on my actual locker–but when I looked, closely, it was there, in invisible ink that was always threatening to bleed through. It was there a little less permanently and publicly in comments fired my way from time to time–ones that I would not have been able to survive had it not been for athletics, as well as the merciful exis-tence of the moderately acceptable category of "tomboy."

---

7. Sure, I thought about taking my beloved vest off for the night, but it would've totally ruined the outfit, and plus, with all of my "busting a move" out there on the dance floor, a faint sweat outline in the shape of the vest had appeared on my Nehru-collared shirt, a situation that presented an entirely different fashion dis-aster with which to contend.
8. As my old therapist would call it.

- When Principal Rooney thinks he's found Ferris Bueller ditching school to do something as banal as play video games at a pizza parlor—it is in fact just a girl who looks like Ferris from behind: tall and thin, short brown hair, wearing that infamous vest (solid black from behind) over a T-shirt, with rolled-up jeans revealing chunky socks and tennis shoes beneath the whole ensemble. When he grabs the kid from behind and she spits soda on him, that was totally me, spinning around and giving Rooney the hairy eyeball, like, "Touch me again and I'll fucking kick you in the nuts so hard you'll be able to take my place with the sopranos in the school choir."
- Even the dopey principal in *The Breakfast Club*, when addressing the group serving detention, derisively calls them all "girls," when there are of course only two "real" girls present (Molly Ringwald and Ally Sheedy).
- "You're a faggot, Blane," spits Steff's girlfriend when Blane dares bring Andie to the party at a "richie's" house in *Pretty in Pink*.
- And of course there's our intro to the decidedly butch Watts (Mary Stuart Masterson) in *SKOW*, when she and Keith are strolling into school and the tough-guy skinhead (Elias Koteas[9]) puts his leg in front of her, prohibiting her from passing:

SKINHEAD: How long have you been a lesbian?

WATTS: Excuse me?

SKINHEAD: I think you have a little bit too much up front to be a guy, so you must be a lesbian.

---

9. Coincidentally a real-life friend of my (much) older brother from when we were growing up. I remember him—the real Elias, not the character of the skinhead—hanging around our house, surfing and skating with my brother and their entirely terrifying group of friends.

A fight of course ensues, where Keith, surely the prettiest art fag[10] in the universe, defends Watts's honor, also getting called a faggot in the process.[11]

These are tiny moments running alongside the main narratives, hardly recognizable because they're simply accurate representations of the requisite, rampant queer-baiting in high schools across the country. But to me, and I'm sure tons of others like me, these moments spoke loudest, and I silently and meticulously cataloged each and every one of them as my "normal" friends and I wore out VHS copies of these movies, making a big to-do about memorizing every cheesy romantic line and all of the intricate choreography involved in every make-out session (in the hay at Blane's country club; on an oil drum in the shop where Keith works as a mechanic; on the football field postdetention when Molly Ringwald gives her diamond stud earring to Judd Nelson, etc.).

Sure, I cared whether Andie ended up with Blane, and if Amanda Jones ever figured out how to stand alone for the "right reasons." But what intrigued me the most were the tertiary characters—the sexually ambiguous (or simply desexualized) best friends who generally get left behind after serving their sole function of funneling the two main love interests[12] together: nerdy Anthony Michael Hall in both *Sixteen Candles* and *The Breakfast Club*; uptight Cameron in *Ferris Bueller*; fey Duckie in *Pretty in Pink*; tomboy Watts in *SKOW*—literally ushering Keith and Amanda Jones around as a driver for hire on the night of their big date. It's not a

10. FYI: Wikipedia (the free encyclopedia) defines "art fag" as "a negative term used in the United States and Canada in the 1980s and 90s to describe passive, introverted, artistic, and/or eccentric teenagers and twentysomethings, and specifically art students. The expression did not actually imply homosexuality but was often used to imply femininity, though the term applied to both males and females. As often happens with derogatory expressions (i.e., queer, nigger, etc.) people who were identified as being 'art fags' have relatively recently started applying it to themselves with pride."

11. The skinhead was obviously not privy to the above definition at the time he employed the "faggot" epithet on the purportedly straight art fag Keith.

12. Who generally exhibit more "normal" sex and gender roles.

coincidence that when Judd Nelson hooks up with Molly Ringwald, and Emilio Estevez with Ally Sheedy, in *The Breakfast Club*, Anthony Michael Hall's character is left with nobody to make out with and is thus shown actually kissing the essay he wrote for the detention assignment. And when Ferris's hot girlfriend strips to go swimming in her Skivvies as Cameron is freaking out about the added mileage on his father's prized Ferrari, he of course gets called out for secretly sneaking peeks at the hot girl (whom he'd presumably never actually be allowed to touch). And of course there's Duckie, who might've ended up with Andie at the end of *Pretty in Pink*, but test audiences obviously thought he was too queer for anything like that, and expressed a strong desire for a union with the "richie" Blane instead. So the ending was reshot accordingly.[13]

I was Duckie, stuck kissing Andie's freaky, older coworker[14] instead of the prize. And I was also Anthony Michael Hall in *Sixteen Candles*, left clutching a pair of panties in my sweaty mitts instead of a real girl who might've been wearing them. Back then I went along with the dominant (hetero)sexuality as it was represented in the films, and so I tried to believe that I simply had crushes on these desexualized guys nobody else seemed to want. They were guys nonetheless, and that's what you were supposed to like . . . I just assumed I had weird taste because I liked these nontraditionally hot boys instead of the more obvious heartthrobs my friends pined for (Andrew McCarthy, James Spader, Emilio Estevez, Craig Sheffer, the birthday cake boy in *Sixteen Candles*, etc.). But as I moved into my twenties and started to figure out my own gender identity,[15] I realized that what I really wanted was to *be* those fey boys–as opposed to being *with* them in any sort of romantic way. An important distinction that became incrementally more clear to me as I grew up.

13. According to the trivia page on the Internet Movie Database and other film fan sites.
14. I don't need to get into it, but he was a teacher at my school.
15. Or figure out that I would probably never completely figure it out.

I know Ferris was the prize, the "normal" and popular kid in the eponymous *Ferris Bueller's Day Off*, but there was also something super gay about him (knowing the lyrics to "Danke Schoen" and wearing that beret? *Please*), and I viewed him as the flip side (on a double-headed coin) of the all-out weirdness of *Pretty in Pink*'s Duckie. The two actors looked strikingly similar at that age, and both address the camera with those sweet, glycerin-enhanced puppy-dog eyes. Both have floppy brown hair, gently rouged cheeks, and a precocious thrift-store aesthetic. And both Ferris and Duckie have those classic scenes where they do what I dreamed of doing (though I didn't know how at the time): They sing (well, lip-synch) to legions of either real or imagined screaming fans. Ferris famously performs "Danke Schoen" and "Twist and Shout" on the German Day parade float on the streets of downtown Chicago; and Duckie dramatically (and queenily) does his little tiptoe dance while mouthing the suggestive lyrics to "Try a Little Tenderness" at Trax for Andie and Iona (substituting a comb for a microphone). *HOT.*

That's what I want to do, I remember sensing deep in my musculature like an ancient memory, but never admitting it to either my friends or myself. Or maybe it just took some time to decipher why the prospect of that kind of performance got me so excited; it wasn't until my early to midtwenties that I started figuring out how I might go about doing it.[16] I had an *Aha* moment one night watching MTV, so naturally, I did the only thing I could possibly do, as soon as I could possibly do it: I started a boy band (the dominant teenage medium for entertainment in the late '90s) and became a professional lip-syncher for a few years. Here I am onstage with my old group, the Backdoor Boys, at a New York club, crooning that ubiquitous bubblegum single "I Want It That Way," by the Backstreet Boys, while the ladies go mad and toss their panties onstage:

---

16. Thanks in part to the gaggle of drag queens I was hanging out with at the time I was living in New Orleans.

© Rachel Daniell

I'm camping it up by soulfully soloing Duckie style, and this is also me in the number 89 jersey in the shot below, from one of our *Teen Beat*– style photo shoots:

© Jocelyn Davis

And yes, if you look close enough at these two images, you'll see that I am literally living out the Ferris-like adolescent boyhood I was never able to have while in high school. Playing the sexually ambiguous card of my own and symbolically joining the ranks of Leif Garrett, Shaun Cassidy, George Michael, Ricky Martin, Justin Timberlake—all the testosterone-challenged singers who make the teenage girls swoon. Singing about wanting to cuddle and talk and share your secrets—not about *nailing* you, like all the smelly, real-life boys pawing you in high school.

So, I was a late bloomer. But I don't mind, because if those were my late teens, then I'm still only in my midtwenties now. And I have John Hughes and his fey boys who were wearing my future to thank for that.

Blowing It

MY *SIXTEEN CANDLES*

By Quinn Dalton

I

I am thirteen, and my family has just moved from South Carolina to Ohio for my father's new job. I've spent the summer working on my tan, religiously watching a new soap opera called *Santa Barbara* (my goal is to see every episode so I'll have current events to discuss at school), and teaching myself how to play the recorder.

In other words, I am bored to the point of profound depression. My eagerness to meet new friends my age overrides my intense fear of having to face a whole new population of eighth graders with my braces, acne, and a bad perm.

Not long after school starts, I see *Sixteen Candles* at the Kent Cinemas with a couple of girls who, in spite of my encyclopedic knowledge of the *Santa Barbara* characters and plotline and my recurring offers to play the recorder for their entertainment, have agreed to be my friends.

A trip to the movies is a major event. I curl my hair, apply multiple coats of lip gloss, and fret about what to wear. I wonder what I'll say if, while I'm gliding down the aisle, a really cute and grown-up high school guy falls for me and asks me out. So of course, a movie like *Sixteen Candles*, with a sweetly nerdy heroine whose unlikely dreams of love are fulfilled to the beat of a synthesized sound track, is made for me. Long before Jake and Sam are sitting on Jake's glass-topped dining table, leaning forward to kiss over her glowing birthday cake, I am awash in the fantasy.

What I don't consider is how the two young lovers find themselves perched there so gracefully. Yes, of course: Jake picks Sam up after her sister's wedding in his red Porsche and whisks her away. But does a high school guy really go buy a cake, stick candles in it, even wipe down the beer-and-puke-crusted table from last night's party, and light the candles without starting a fire? And what are the chances of climbing up there without smearing icing all over your clothes, breaking through the glass, or burning off your eyebrows?

No matter—I feel sure that I will have a romantic, humiliation-free moment like this if I can just survive the next three years. I have decided that I want to be Molly Ringwald, with her short-in-the-back, tousled-on-top boyish hairdo, her jaunty vests and pink crop tops. I know in an epiphanic sort of way that I need some paisley in my wardrobe.

My two friends and I go back to see the movie again the following weekend. This time another scene sticks out for me. Jake is working out in the gym with a huge, thuggy jock played by an actor who must be thirty-five—though this probability escapes me, along with the fact that the actors playing Jake (Michael Schoeffling) and his sexy cheerleader girlfriend, Caroline (Haviland Morris), are both in their midtwenties.

In the gym Jake is thinking about Sam after intercepting a note Sam passed to a friend in a class they have together, child development (did anyone ever take child development in high school?). In the note Sam had written that if she were to "do it" with anyone, her choice would be none other than Jake Ryan himself. Between pull-ups in the gym, Jake asks his thug friend what he thinks of Sam.

The thug looks disgusted and says, "I don't."

A couple of lines later Jake says moodily, "She's not ugly."

This epitome of the backhanded compliment pierces me. I am white-knuckled from my grip on the armrests. I am remembering how, earlier that week, a boy from my homeroom called me a dog, loudly, in front of the whole class. This in spite of my diligent tanning regimen, maintained even with the ever-present lake effect (which I will later learn is northeastern Ohio's handy explanation for nearly everything, not just the frequently cloudy weather—bad drivers, the recession, serial killers lurking under cars in mall parking lots, waiting to slice your Achilles tendon). The class fell silent, waiting for my response. I was too stunned to say anything.

All I know by then is that not to be considered ugly might be the best I can hope for.

II

Three years later I wake on the morning of my sixteenth birthday in a hotel double bed in Toronto next to my mother. In the other double bed, against the wall, my father and younger brother snore. Our trip coincides with a conference my father is attending, but it has been repackaged as a Sweet-Sixteen Birthday Tour, since recent events have convinced my parents that they can never again let me out of their sight.

The problem centers on my first serious boyfriend, F., a just-graduated senior, though a bit too blond, bespectacled, and into Pink Floyd to be considered your Jake Ryan type. But I know that I am in love with him, and he has professed his love for me. Unfortunately, my parents have made me break up with him because my mother accidentally-on-purpose overheard me telling a friend on the phone about how F. and I had rented a hotel room on prom night a few weeks earlier.

It was supposed to be the Big Night. We thought we could get away with it because my mother and father were on a trip to Italy (their first trip overseas and, as it turned out, the only trip they ever took of any length while I lived with them).

My parents had left my brother and me in the custody of a graduate student of my father's who was perhaps too distracted for the job, as she was in the last throes of a relationship with a tepid engineering candidate who wore sideburns and wasn't going to marry her, and maybe because of all this she politely overlooked the fact that I did not come home on prom night. However, my mother had other spies; she maintained that she had been supplied with a photocopy of F.'s signature in the hotel's guest register—*He was stupid enough to write his own name?* I thought, frantically, in the living room when my parents informed me of their findings.

Since then, and leading up to the Toronto trip, my mother has threatened to use the incriminating evidence to press charges against him for statutory rape (as he turned eighteen right before prom) should I ever attempt to see him again.

Staring at the little red maple leaves dotting the hotel-room drapes on the morning of the birthday I've been anticipating for so long, the birthday that was supposed to involve dinner on the marina in Cleveland with F., maybe a boat ride through the Flats, and yes, sixteen candles, I think of the candlelit cake scene with Jake and Sam. It occurs to me that the real dream of the movie is not just winning the rich, hot, seven-years-older-than-your-average-high-school-senior guy. It is the freedom that comes with a family so preoccupied with their oldest daughter's wedding that they don't even remember your birthday.

III

After being forced to end my first real romance, I wonder for a string of miserable months if I'll ever find love again. Or, more accurately, at all, because it has occurred to me that I wasn't so much in love with F. as I was curious—about what a boy felt like and what it sounds like to hear yourself say breathlessly, dramatically, "I love you."

But there I am the following spring, prom night again, wearing a red off-the-shoulder gown with a flouncy layered skirt, looking adoringly up at B. My bangs are curled in a sort of sausage roll across my forehead, and my hair is swept up in back with a red satin flower barrette. I wear a fake pearl choker and dangly matching earrings for which my mother and I shopped for hours. B. looks dashing in his black tuxedo with tails, and seeing as how we are so above the matching-dress-and-cummerbund so popular among promgoers, his is black. His tie is skewed at the same angle as the line of his hair, which dips over his right eye with a little flip like a tilted hat.

I smile primly for every picture my father takes of us in the living room. One shows us standing in profile, gazing straight ahead; you can tell we're working at looking beautiful and pensive. My neck is no thicker than my upper arm.

In about three months B. will have broken up with me, gently as he is able, because he will have started college in a farm town just over an hour's drive away from Kent, but it will feel as remote as China.

But on that night we walk into a fancy French restaurant in the Cuyahoga Valley for dinner before the prom, and we pass a man and a woman who are just leaving. They are probably in their fifties, older than my parents at the time. The woman has bleached-blond hair and an orange tan. She smiles at us, the white crescents around her eyes crinkling. The man—beefy, red-faced—shifts a toothpick from one corner of his mouth to the other. He glances at us, shakes his head, and says after we are already behind them, "They're so young. No one deserves to be that young."

But I want to deserve it. So I tell myself to try to remember this, how other people could see some kind of magic in us, even for one night. I decide to see this as a sign that our evening is completely charmed, and that by extension B. and I are charmed. I decide that this is my birthday after all, the sweet sixteenth one, where candles are lit by an unseen hand and cakes and lovers appear to float.

IV

I think a part of you is still in love with your first love, always. This is the one you walked into clean—with empty pockets and no past— when you were too young to worry about your career, or whether there might be children or a divorce tucked away somewhere. You haven't yet tested—and discovered—your own limits, or anyone else's, for that matter. This is when you create the universe of love you will live in for the rest of your life. You will measure other, future, more complicated, more mature loves against it.

You will of course change. You will want different things from a partner. You will come to a place in your life, probably quite soon, when you can no longer imagine yourself matched with the person who meant so much to you back then. But you will still want yourself from those days, when you were younger than you deserved, when you didn't even think to ask, "What next?"

I mean, did I really believe Sam and Jake would end up married? That final scene didn't even want me to ask the question. And I obliged; I suspended my curiosity about their future as effortlessly as they seemed suspended on that glass table.

But here's my guess: They'll have a great year together. They'll "do it." Jake will leave for college—he'll get in somewhere good based on his father's connections. He'll break up with Sam. Maybe by then Farmer Ted will have filled out a little. Or maybe Sam won't even consider him until she runs into him years later, in a restaurant, or at a conference, and Farmer Ted is pulling down the big bucks, having recently IPO'd his first dot-com. Meanwhile, Jake will have snorted away his father's money. He'll be selling insurance, not trying to hide his gut anymore. He will hear a woman refer to him as "not ugly," and he'll take it as a compliment.

V

I caught *Sixteen Candles* on cable late one night recently and sat through the whole thing. Twenty years later I was most compelled by the peripheral characters—the ones I wasn't supposed to care about; the ones that were planted for laughs—like the racist joke that was Long Duk Dong, and the girl in the neck brace, an early appearance by Joan Cusack, who kept dousing herself at the water fountain or tipping backward out of her chair.

I guess Neck Brace Girl was supposed to take the fall for all of us—for every time you slipped and fell on your ass on an ice patch right in front of the school bus, every time you drooled food onto your shirt because your braces had just been tightened. At least you weren't *handicapped*, to use the '80s term—or worse, an Asian exchange student with a not-so-good command of English.

And then there was Caroline, Jake's girlfriend, screwing Farmer Ted after the dance. Of course, she was passed out, drunk, but she was pretty sure it happened and she'd enjoyed it! The only detail I could recall about her character from my previous viewings was that she'd had the back of her hair cut off to get unstuck from a door. (You want to freak out a teenage girl, threaten to cut off a chunk of her hair.) This time I was more struck by the idea that an unconscious girl could enjoy sex with a guy she wouldn't have spoken to the day before.

From my thirteen-year-old's perspective, it didn't matter if Caroline knew what she was doing. Sex in your boyfriend's daddy's Rolls-Royce with a near stranger? No big deal! I mean, it wasn't, like, her first time. The movie wanted me to enjoy her dismantling, her fall from bitchy goddess to bedraggled geek conquest.

But now, as a thirty-four-year-old mother of two girls, I saw it a little differently. I wanted to put my arm around Caroline and take her home. I wanted to tell her that however old she felt right then, she was really quite young. I wanted to say I understood why she had pretended to enjoy what she couldn't remember, because it couldn't be undone.

There was another moment that got my attention on this last viewing, when Sam and Farmer Ted are sitting in a partially disassembled car in the shop room during the dance, and Sam says to Farmer Ted, "You could come back next year as a completely normal person."

Perhaps, more than anything, that's the dream I was living for during the era that *Sixteen Candles* depicted in crass slapstick and moments of humor and insight. I kept hoping I might somehow magically become a completely normal person through the way that I styled my hair or practiced walking down aisles or thought of myself in love. I was trying to prepare myself to reflect, and then become, that young woman, whenever she arrived.

Can't Help Falling in Love

by Emily Franklin

I.

The lights dim, making my bright blue leggings and braces, my home-cut bobbed hair, fade into the darkness of the movie theater. I'm in eighth grade–the only thing worse than this passing situation is that rather than being with a boyfriend (which I've never had), I am with my mother.

The Suzanne Vega song "Left of Center" plays, and I watch Molly Ringwald on-screen as Andie in *Pretty in Pink*, a girl who–despite her banged-up purple car and homemade lacy outfits–has not one but three guys who like her. Couples are scattered around me and my mother, their kisses punctuating the on-screen romance. Their interlocked fingers seem the height of love. The fact that red-headed, full-lipped, quirky Andie has so much male attention thrust her way doesn't seem far-fetched to me at the time; of course it's natural for the rich, hot Steff to have lusty, unanswered longings for her, and of course it makes sense that Duckie, her longtime best friend, secretly pines for her, and why shouldn't bland Blane return her crush feelings? She is, after all, bespectacled, poor, offbeat (which is often the kiss of social death at high school), and smart.

After the movie lets out, I am left with two key ideas. One is a fantasy–that girls who fly low under the radar are wonderful, hidden gems, secretly appreciated by all manner of boys. The other is more my reality–having a guy best friend makes sense. I am too young, at just thirteen, to know that years of befriending my own Duckies are ahead.

"What'd you think?" my mother asks as we weave through the throngs of teenagers, many with their hands still clasped.

"I loved it," I say. I touch my hair, wondering if I, too, can pull off hats set at a jaunty angle, or lace stockings, or wire-rimmed glasses though my eyesight is fine. My mother looks at me as we get into the car.

"He really liked her," she says.

"Andrew McCarthy? I know." I'm already recalling the amazing and (in my mind) impossible way he and Andie communicated by typing onto the computer screen.

"No, not him," my mother says as she gets behind the wheel. "The other boy—her friend. He really liked her." She turns the key and pulls the car into the lot, near other cars jammed with kids and friends who seem to me—just by being a few years older and part of a couple—to be inhabitants of a world that feels far away. "Your father and I were best friends."

I nod. I know this story—of how my parents met at thirteen and became friends, then dated, then married. I'm exactly that age now. Might I already know my future mate? This idea of marrying your best friend has been handed down as lore, as the best idea, the slogan of marriage—the way it should be.

"So you think she should have wound up with Duckie?" I quickly rewrite the scene at the prom when Duckie appears all tricked out in his alterna-tuxedo and admires Andie's off-the-shoulder pink number. What if they'd kissed then instead of going off with their less-platonic dates?

But rather than give an emphatic nod, my mother sighs. "That Andrew McCarthy is dreamy." We drive the rest of the way in silence, and I rush up to my room to see if, after viewing *Pretty in*

Pink, I have suddenly acquired my own sewing skills that will help me create an outfit so spectacular that I am propelled from my current status as the girl guys can talk to, to the one they want to go out with.

II.

A year-plus later, and not even my faded jeans and loosely draped scarf can hide the fact that while I may dress like the typical private high schooler in the Northeast, I'm still not in *that* crowd. I'm a floater; not exactly popular, not a social castoff, not really one thing or another. I am not enough of any particular group (jock, hottie, stoner, preppy, nerd) to commit fully to joining. Instead I form friendships that exist cross-culturally in the high school sense—I'm friends with seniors though I'm a freshman, I hang out with boarders though I'm a day student, I take Chinese instead of French or Spanish like everyone else, I'm nice to computer kids and golden girls alike, and I become friends with boys.

The first is K., lanky and loose-limbed, who appreciates the absurdity of being this age and makes me laugh all through study hall. Ours is an intense friendship filled with long phone calls and quickly scrawled notes passed in class, assuring each other we'll meet outside the dining-hall doors and eat lunch together. My mother is the first to bring to my attention that K. may not just be in this for kicks. "So, do you like him, too?" she asks after she's made me hang up the phone.

I shake my head to prove she's all wrong. "No—it's not like that. He doesn't like me like *that* . . . we're just friends."

But of course my mother is correct. All that crush debauchery from my teen movies can't dispel the truth. By the close of the winter play (in which, to my dismay, I am cast as a warrior queen because, according to the director, I have the *strength* to play her—

though in my fantasies I am lithe and cute enough to play the other heroines, one of whom gets to kiss K.), K. insists we "try it out." This loosely translates into a make-out session at the cast party. In the attic we grope a little and he kisses me, even though I have doubts. Sure enough, the kiss doesn't work—at least not for me—and I push away, only to find out that rejecting K.'s advances results in the end of our friendship. Within a week he's dating an older girl—a tenth grader—and I am back to flying low under the dating radar.

III.

When I see *Some Kind of Wonderful*, I am older than my *Pretty in Pink* days. Old enough to know that clothing probably isn't magically going to make the guy like me, but young enough that my father both drives and accompanies me. We sit next to each other watching Eric Stoltz lust after Lea Thompson's impossibly thin body while Mary Stuart Masterson pines for him. When they wind up together at the end, I think about my mother's dictum, "Thou shalt marry your best friend." It makes perfect sense, I think, but the reality isn't quite so easy.

Watts and Keith remind me of every male-female friendship I have then. Either I want him as more than a friend but he doesn't know it, or else, though I don't quite believe it, he likes me. Aside from drooling over Eric Stoltz's Keith and his shaggy head of copper hair, his sensitivity and drawing skills, I find myself relating to Watts. The truth is we're nothing alike: She has Charlie Brown–style absent parents, while mine are around—next to me, in fact; she's edgy, and I'm not; I want to do well in school, and she's a rebel; she's from the wrong side of the tracks (shown so blatantly with real train tracks that, even at fourteen, I roll my eyes), and I'm from the respectable part of town. In fact, my town has no wrong side. But then there's the longing. Like Molly Ringwald in *Sixteen Candles* crushing on Jake Ryan and his cow eyes. Like Molly Ringwald in *The Breakfast Club* finding herself drawn, against her better judgment, to loner Judd Nelson and his pierced ear. Like Molly Ringwald in *Pretty in Pink* liking passionless but palatable Andrew McCarthy from afar. I feel for Watts as she bangs her heart-adorned drums. I seem to relate to her on a cellular level. Her despair comes through in each beat, and I write lengthy entries in my journal. I write poems and stories and wish for the start of things, for love, for something to happen.

"She's so pretty," Dad says afterward.

"Lea Thompson?" I ask, remembering the locker-room scene where her rail-thin body is on display. I don't own string-bikini underwear and cannot fathom going to a boy's house when his parents aren't home. Not so much because I wouldn't want to, but because I haven't been asked.

"No–the other one. The friend."

"Mary Stuart Masterson," I confirm. "Yeah–I'm glad they wound up together."

"He chose her," Dad says. "It's a decision."

I think about this that night and for months afterward. Watts and Keith have been friends for years presumably, and yet somehow their connection morphs to where she likes him so much she can't take it anymore. When Keith tells her he's going on a date with Amanda, Watts takes it upon herself to teach her friend how to kiss. I replay that particular scene in my mind, wishing I had a friend like that–someone I loved being with platonically but whose lips I also wanted on mine.

Unfortunately, it's often mutually exclusive. N. and I share witty banter and strange humor that involves writing stories and speaking in a language only the two of us seem able to follow. I'm oblivious to his feelings until, after several years, he spills them in a letter. Simultaneous to this is my friendship with E., whom I discover I have a crush on, while he makes me mix tapes that disguise his feelings in songs. But E. doesn't feel the same by the time I'm clued in. So I've got N., who likes me but whom I just can't picture kissing, and E., whose lips I want to kiss but who's now at college, while I'm stuck in the last year of high school. I want to reenact the kissing scene between Watts and Keith, to prove friendship can cross those lines, succeed with diamond earrings and professed love, but by the time E. and I try it, the moment's passed. And when I finally decide I could–might–like kissing N., he's long gone at college; discovered as the university catch, and is unavailable for dating, having been caught underneath an actress.

IV.

At the gym I work out while watching a Hughes film festival: *Sixteen Candles, Pretty in Pink, The Breakfast Club, Some Kind of Wonderful*. I watch them all over the course of a week and meditate on what has stuck with me twenty years after first viewing.

In *Sixteen Candles*, Jake Ryan was that boy, the senior I liked but couldn't have, the junior I liked but couldn't have, any boy who didn't notice me–not because I was a sophomore, but because I didn't fit with whatever style was acceptable at the moment. I had ten pounds that showed up primarily in my breasts; rather than making the most of this, I hid in baggy tops. I liked worn-in T-shirts, not blouses. I preferred reading to parties. Or maybe I just wasn't comfortable with my left-of-center status. Perhaps it is easier to be slightly out of focus when your teenage style suggests difference: the girl with the shaved head in my class, for example, or the one who wore fishnets without irony–they didn't fly under the radar, they were purposefully different. I was different by accident. Jake doesn't

ask Sam to the prom, doesn't lend her his Porsche or confess his
love—he just picks her up after her sister's wedding and gives her a
birthday cake.

During the one blessed year my parents got cable in the eighties, I watched this movie a dozen times—often out of sequence. Only
the end mattered to me—she gets the guy, the one guy she doesn't
know and yet would consent to losing her virginity to, and he magically knows what to get her to make her wish come true. At the time
I held a microphone up to the television speaker to record the
scene—the dialogue, yes, but mainly the song in the background, "If
You Were Here" by Thompson Twins.

Pretty in Pink had "If You Leave." *A lot of "if's,"* I think as I
sweat it out on the elliptical while watching Blane's one act of
ardency: kissing Andie in the parking lot. My mother was right—of
course—Duckie was the way to go. His charm, his humor, his sheer
devotion to Andie and her terrible clothing. Had I really wanted to
sew a dress like that? Did I actually cut arms off of my grandmother's dress from the thirties and try to modernize it with a bow
like Andie did? Sadly, yes. But even my mother had conflict—
Duckie had character and conviction, but oh that Andrew
McCarthy, damn his good looks and blazers.

I watch the women at the gym huffing and puffing and smiling
as they revisit the movies of yore. Each of us clings to a specific
one—a certain heroine who pulled us in, made us okay in our
back-then personas, or informed us whom we might become. So
badly did I want to experience the John Hughes version of reality
that I wished my school had detention. None of the characters in
The Breakfast Club felt like me, though in watching it, I had
instant hope that social change was as easy as a headband and a
swipe of mascara from the popular girl. Ally Sheedy emerges
white-dressed and pretty, having shed her old heap of malcontent

with her black clothes. This sticks with me as I watch it now, that ease of becoming.

With *Some Kind of Wonderful*, I return with mixed feelings. Whereas my teenage self thought Keith was cute, and related to Watts and her confusing love for her best friend, my adult self sees the film differently. Keith likes Amanda Jones, the hottest girl in school, the one who is mistreated by but coupled with the hottest guy. He's not sparring with Amanda, or hanging out with her and slowly finding himself drawn to her–he just wants her. And Watts–pretty, but in a way that perhaps only people like my dad, people with perspective like I have now, admire–honestly adores Keith. Why doesn't he see it for so long? Because he wants to believe in the myth of Amanda Jones and her colt legs, that inside the closed circle of the cool kids is a place for all of us. And why doesn't Watts tell him? Because she is afraid she'll lose him.

I lost several of those mixed friendships–K., N., and E., in high school, S. in college, and F. in graduate school–all of those feelings that emerged over the course of years and months only to find we were mismatched or have the feelings fade. My husband and I met, became best friends, and married within four months. Looking at this whirlwind now, I wonder if perhaps I was circumventing the system I created–beating the odds of transferring friendship to romance.

This past year I cleaned out the last of my boxes from my mother's house. It felt like the ultimate act of adulthood. Beyond having children, beyond marriage, past house buying–everything I own is now under my roof. I discarded many of the items–notes from seventh grade, posters of *Harold and Maude* and *Howard the Duck*, rhinestone brooches, a pastel Swatch that died long ago, letters from people whose names mean nothing. Then, amid the clump of past and the smell of mildew, I found my old wallet–red and navy, sporty, with a stripe of Velcro for closure. Inside it was empty, save for one item: a black-and-white *Some Kind of Wonderful* business card that depicted Keith, Watts, and Amanda in the triangle formation of the film's focus. This I kept.

I still have the film sound tracks, and sometimes, when I'm alone in my minivan, I play the now-warbly tapes. *Some Kind of Wonderful*'s was my favorite. I remember my father thought "Can't Help Falling in Love" was sung by Lick the Thames (we lived in London then, and he thought the idea of licking that polluted water was disgusting). Really, it's Lick the Tins, which may be just as bad a name for a band, but the song still drums up feelings of hope—that cloying pennywhistle, the sweet potential of love in the future. Maybe I believed that love was out of your control. It could invade a friendship, change a moment, and you had to go with it.

I sing "Turn to the Sky" and "Miss Amanda Jones" and think about the girl I was when I first watched that movie. I had no idea then how many friendship fumbles lay ahead for me, how much longing was in store. Agog, I studied Watts and how she wrapped her legs around Keith, teaching him to kiss, hoping somehow to transfer from her lips to his the notion that friendship and love were meant to be combined. At the time I was sure I was Watts, the one doing the convincing. But when I see my track record—the skidded friendships and attempted kisses, the mistimed crushes from me to a boy, from him back to me—it seems that it was the other way around. I was the girl who didn't quite fit in, who wasn't quick to be noticed, who thought she could pick and choose when and how and who. I was the one who needed the right kiss to hook me in, to explain that love could be familiar, that it didn't require reinvention in the form of a makeover, a pink dress, or diamond earrings. I knew what I wanted. Maybe Jake Ryan got it right after all. His offer was simple: just a wish, nothing more—nothing less.

Pretty in Penury

by Lisa Gabriele

When I was young and knew nothing about money, I believed what our priest told us about the rich: that they were bad, that they'd go to hell, and that though they might have it good here on Earth, later, under the lash of the devil, they'd know suffering just like us poor folks. He said something to that effect, probably under the auspices of paraphrasing Jesus. So I grew up a little afraid of the rich and their godless insouciance. But that didn't stop me from wanting to live among them, to be one of them, even if it meant eternal damnation. Not too long after that I stopped asking God to bless my mommy and daddy in my prayers and started asking him for cold, hard cash.

I'm from the "other side of the tracks," a place much like the street in the opening shot of *Pretty in Pink*. The pan of those squat, unremarkable homes, stacked side by side like rotting teeth, reminds me of the one-streetlight town near an ugly, blue-collar city where I was raised. All the saltbox houses were surrounded by chain-link fences, behind which messy toddlers wandered shirtless and upset, one hand up their nose, the other holding up their saggy diaper. If you had ambitions, you were scoffed at. Some mothers had part-time jobs, maybe at the arena, maybe taking in other people's kids, the extra money possibly affording them an aboveground pool or a trip to Florida to see some relatives. While they unpacked their Ping-Pong tables or showed off their Siamese cats ("She's the indoor-only kind!"), my mother would mutter about them behind their backs. Who did they think they were, with their salon perms and their campers, smoking their menthol cigarettes on their new decks, hovering above the rest of us like they thought they were so good? What, did they think they were rich or something?

As I got older, I learned that others had what I wanted, and so I became rabidly, unflatteringly covetous. Whenever we drove by mansions, I'd picture my distracted mother pulling our rusty station wagon over in front of the U-shaped driveway. "Well, nice to see you people. Do take care," I'd imagine yelling to the depressed cargo, before breaking into a sprint at the bend, following the sounds of chamber music and corgis echoing off the sun-dappled roof of my *real* family's home. "Oh Christ, quit talking fancy," my mother would always reply in the daydream, shattering the rest of it by tossing her spent cigarette into the mansion's pristine hedges. Acting fancy was a sin to my mother unless someone better than you (read: rich) was pinning a carnation to your homemade prom dress or wrestling a half-carat diamond ring over your knocked-up knuckle.

I must make this distinction: We weren't poor as in hungry, we were poor as in broke and tacky. To me, it was worse than being hungry because middle-class comforts were dangled right before my eyes. I could see them, almost touch them, but did not have them because my parents couldn't afford them. Their crowd spent their money on cigarettes, bingo, and beer, so I grew up ashamed not just of being poor, but also of the bad taste and manners that seemed to go with the lifestyle. And I vowed to get out.

That's why *Pretty in Pink* (incidentally, only written by John Hughes) was such a revelation. It showed me my world. And though I occupied it with less grace and sartorial imagination than did Molly Ringwald's Andie, I carried her chronic shame. Like Andie, I didn't bear the mantel of our poverty with stoicism. It enraged me. And my parents' depressing acceptance of "our lot" became the fuel that stoked my considerable ambitions. Before *Pretty in Pink* I'd seen class issues portrayed in films, but I'd rarely seen poor people who looked like me, at least not in the contemporary movies I lined up to see.

In high school, teenagers become aware that they are held hostage by their family's socioeconomic status. After all, you live with these people. If they're poor and unemployable, as in the case of Andie's father, played by the poetically hungover Harry Dean Stanton, then so are you. When Andie wakes her father for a job interview, she says, "Come on, this means a lot to me." Not only do they need the money, but sitting around in his undershirt on the front lawn drinking beer with Duckie is beginning to reflect badly on her, too.

Andie is smart enough to be "allowed," as she puts it, to attend the rich kids' high school, but it is there that her otherness is made daily apparent. In one class (the topics: Marxism, the New Deal, and the Emergency Banking Act) her snooty, rich classmates tease her about the uniqueness of her vintage outfit. They suggest its history implies a certain kind of cheapness, and while Andie's ironic punk sensibility completely eludes them, her pride doesn't. Later, when her crush, Blane, comes to her store to buy a record, at first she's thrilled to see him. But Andie can't help asking him if he'll be paying with an American Express Platinum Card, bitter sarcasm licking the edges of her words. Her face beautifully expresses that awful dichotomy of hating the thing you want, or maybe it's wanting the thing you hate. Either way, Andie suddenly realizes that to date Blane is to betray her tribe, to shun her world and perhaps leave behind her real friends. She's tormented by the decision. As for me, I couldn't wait to say "See ya."

Unlike Andie's, some of my friends were from wealthy families. They lived in those same mansions Andie and Duckie eye on their ride home from the nightclub. The first mansion I imagined living in was the local private high school. It was the opposite of our clapboard hovel, which was in the kind of neighborhood that considered the local perv eccentric, where people thought curfews hung in windows, and ferrets were pets. Saint Mary's Academy, by contrast, was covered in ivy and set back from the road on two acres of velveteen grass. I imagined nestling in a window box sketching wildlife, like a girl on the cover of a get-well card. Wandering my friends' fancy houses, I didn't covet the chintz couches or stainless-steel appliances (let alone a basic dishwashing machine), I marveled at the idea of ornamental soap, cut flowers, and the salted mixed nuts—the good kind, minus peanuts—which were cradled in crystal bowls strewn about the house. I loved that people had towels that were for "guests," whoever they were. (The concept of having guests was exotic, our house too overcrowded and messy for such social banalities. Plus, we were related mostly to other poor people, and they don't travel much.)

Sure, I wanted my friends' Nikes or New Balance shoes, their Le Sportsac purses and Esprit sweaters. But what really made me dizzy with envy was their routines. They practiced piano after school and took makeup application courses at Sears. At a certain time, and every evening, their not previously frozen dinners would appear on matching plates alongside matching cutlery. If I was invited for dinner, I rarely stayed. I couldn't guarantee that I wouldn't gulp down the food in embarrassingly ravenous bites, not because I was hungry, but because the abundance seemed bottomless. That's also where Andie and I differ. While I regarded those homes with the subtlety of a cross-eyed Romanian orphan, Andie regards them affectionately, with an expression that seems almost homesick. She doesn't wish she lived in one of them so much as she seems surprised that she doesn't.

As soon as humanly possible, I did what Andie did; I got a part-time job. Mine wasn't in a cool record store, but rather, a pricey steak house, one my family could not afford to patronize. After my dad left for good, we teetered on total penury. Five of us shared a two-bedroom rental. My mother worked several jobs, collapsing each night onto the foldout in the living room. But for three shifts a week at the steak house I could pretend I was a member of the middle-to-upper class. The restaurant gave me a uniform to care for, a list of rules to follow, a philosophy to memorize, and a tradition to uphold. I was part of the restaurant's family, so I began to have much less to do with my own. Though my real family was happy I had found work I loved, they dismissed the information I shared with them over supper. I often felt like I was talking to a table of deaf Vikings when I explained that steak should be cooked medium rare, not blackened and attached to T-bones. Vegetables deserved to be steamed just shy of crunchy, never uncanned and boiled to a pudding in buttery water. Pitchers served fastballs, people, not beer! And salad dressing could be formed from a multitude of fresh ingredients, not just spanked out of a sticky bottle. I was becoming the worst kind of snob, the kind without money.

At first my paycheck went almost entirely to clothing, whatever was in, whatever the rich girls were wearing, anything to keep the awful shame of being poor at bay. The designer labels acted as an armor, protecting me from my wealthy peers' judgment. Not that it happened much. The rich kids I knew were too blithe and happy for that kind of cruelty. So while my mother might have filed for bankruptcy, and we might have had Kraft dinner for the fourth night in a row, at school, away from our shoddy street, I looked like a million bucks. Or at least a couple hundred thou.

Pretty in Pink was also my generation's *Annie Hall*, igniting in me and others I knew a lifelong love affair with used, vintage, or repurposed clothing. I used to shorten my mother's '50s plaid skirts, rip the sleeves off blouses and tie them in front, and cut my brothers' jeans into floor-length hippie skirts. I was known for having a quirky, creative style, and it became another way to distract people from my poverty. But there's an irony to wearing vintage. Andie's outfits, set off by fedoras and pearls, are from bygone eras that reflect her old-fashioned values: that hard work, honesty, and loyalty might one day garner her a good life. But at the same time the outfits represent a big "Fuck you" to that notion. Because by the eighties hard work, honesty, and loyalty–especially, say, to a corporation–guaranteed you nothing. Witness Andie's father, a man Ronald Reagan's policies practically created: the disenfranchised, middle-aged victim of trickle-down economics and depression. That's also why I was saddened when Iona, Andie's punk, funny boss, sells out her singular style to date the yuppie pet-store guy. Annie Potts is utterly marvelous in this movie, her acting worthy of a supporting-actress award, or at least a nomination. As a woman who's closer to Iona's age now, I see how Potts really nails that combination of feeling both nostalgic for youth while recoiling from the idea of reliving it. And when Andie tells Iona she's going to the prom, Potts's response, "I envy you," is infused with just the right amount of love. It's impossible to imagine another actress in the role. Andie's relationship with Iona also reminds me of all the maternal crushes I'd get on my cool female bosses, the ones who had raucous love lives and a bit of a drinking problem. I took my cues on how to be a woman from them, my own mother being too overwhelmed and too depressed to provide many useful hints.

As for Harry Dean Stanton, he breaks my heart as Andie's unemployed, single dad. He doesn't quite fit. He's almost a little too sexy/seedy in the role. And even though there's genuine affection between the characters, I've always felt that they were in two different movies, his taking place in a dusty border town and hers in Hughes's natural habitat, Chicago. But still, it works because their scenes are always authentic, especially the one when Andie arrives home overjoyed about being asked to the prom by Blane. Though I'm not sure about Stanton's shorty bathrobe or how he tugs the front part down as he crosses his legs on the couch, I love their rapport. She gets to be a vulnerable daughter in this scene and not his constant caretaker.

When you're poor, dating is complicated. You don't want guys to know you're poor. They will think you are desperate. They will also think your poverty has perverted your morals; hence, they will think you're easy. That's why my heart seized at the scene where Andie tells Blane to pick her up at the mall for their date. I had done that so many times, the mall acting as a neutral ground where our disparate classes could meet and mingle. And even if I was being judged by what I bought, fact is, at least I was buying something.

I remember a date with a guy named Peter whose father was a doctor. They had money. They had class. They lived in one of the most secluded and exclusive neighborhoods in the city. They had an indoor pool, plus a Jacuzzi in the master suite. They even paid other people to mow the lawn. Meanwhile, we had moved to a tiny rental four doors down from the most dangerous tavern in the county. Weekends my younger sister and brother tended the bar underage and cultivated regulars with names such as Snow Monkey, Biker Pete, Rye and Ginger (a couple), and Old Jake, who drank until his piss-stained corduroys could no longer grip the barstool. Despite the job's mortal danger, my mother was thrilled because now her younger children could buy their own cigarettes instead of always stealing hers. My family's mentality made it hard for me to imagine a boy pulling up our gravel driveway clutching a corsage. So Peter picked me up for my date at the mall.

After dinner, for which he paid, he brought me back to his house. It was empty of parents. There he made several futile attempts to have sex with me. Eventually I told him to take me home. I was no prude, nor was I a virgin, but I was pretty sure he didn't treat other girls like that. It seemed he had no intention of making me his girlfriend. So I let him drive me right to the front steps of our rental, and he did not offer to walk me to the door. Imagining that our new neighborhood frightened him gave me small comfort.

He never called again.

Blane's appeal has always eluded me, but I find Steff's predatory flirtations with Andie infuriatingly sexy. Andie accuses him of just wanting sex, though Steff counters by saying he wants something more meaningful, the same lie I fell for again and again. Who knows, maybe they meant it. But I always got my heart broken in high school by guys like Steff, guys who knew no matter what they said and did, below them was the safety net of their parents' money, which, to me, was more exotic than ritual cannibalism or voodoo-chanting Gypsies. I deeply crushed on boys who possessed that sense of security. It was never about the money or their nice cars; it was about their confidence, the way they seemed to walk the earth like they'd invented it. It was years before I understood the difference between confidence and arrogance, and that Steff loved Andie because, unlike him and the girls he dated, she had an enormous amount of self-respect. You can see that when their eyes meet outside of the school, just before Andie confronts Blane about the cowardly way he pulls out of the prom. It's also one of the hottest moments in the whole movie, even hotter than Blane and Andie's kiss, or Duckie's dance in the record store. That's largely due to James Spader's incredible carnality, and perhaps partially due to the fact that he was in his midtwenties in the film. Steff practically hate-fucks her with his eyes.

Watching *Pretty in Pink* all these years later, I am reminded of what Andie has that I didn't. I was rejected over and over again in high school, not because I was poor or from the wrong side of the tracks. I was dumped because I was ashamed of those things. I knew then and certainly know now that the rich have no monopoly on self-respect. In fact, in most of John Hughes's movies money indicates the absence of respect. The "richies," as Andie calls Blane and his ilk, are depicted as spiritually bankrupt, morally vacuous, debauched, spoiled addicts. Steff is never without a cigarette, a drink, or a joint in his hand. After Blane calls him on his bad behavior, Steff's given the best line in the movie: "Would I treat my parents' house like this if money was any kind of issue?"

Even Blane is exposed as a flawed sellout, a guy who rejects Andie when he's threatened with social ostracism. In *Pretty in Pink*, Hughes is telling us that it's not money, clothes, and boys that bring us happiness. Love, honesty, and integrity are far greater commodities. And Andie knows this.

But the most powerful scene in the movie is when Andie loudly excoriates Blane at the lockers, accusing him of being ashamed to take her to the prom. It's still so enlivening, so transfixing, to see a beautifully enraged teenage girl, one who's not covered in pig's blood, track marks, or Prada. I replay that scene over and over the way my brothers might replay the finale of *Hoosiers*. It's Molly Ringwald's finest moment in the film and, I would suggest, her career. She teeters on ugly, her face contorting with visceral disgust for Blane, which is why the ending, reportedly reshot with Blane instead of Duckie as the victorious suitor, feels inauthentic to me. I never believed that Andie would forgive so easily after that humiliation, dropping her purse on the ground in their passionate parking-lot kiss.

That said, I carry that redheaded girl in my heart to this day. I carry her pride and her unassuming beauty, her integrity and her ingenuity. Andie Walsh was everything I could not be back then because I was mired in epic self-pity. But Andie demonstrates there is freedom in self-love, because you can't be victimized by other people's opinions or labels when your core is solid and impenetrable, and when you know you're loved by those who matter. In fact, after all these years I can honestly say that I still want to be like Andie Walsh when I grow up.

That's Not a Name, That's a Major Appliance

HOW ANDREW McCARTHY RUINED MY LIFE

by Tod Goldberg

Andrew McCarthy isn't a very large man, and his face belies no clear evidence that he's aware of my boiling hatred of him, nor that for the last twenty years I've wished a variety of painful skin diseases on him, so I find his lack of physical size rather comforting. Never mind that Andrew McCarthy is standing in front of me because he's doing me a huge favor by lending his acting skills to the reading of a short story of mine before an audience of oxymorons: Hollywood Literary Hipsters. And never mind that I am aware that Andrew McCarthy is not, in fact, Blane McDonough from *Pretty in Pink*; that he is a working actor and that he has played plenty of other characters. The fact that Andrew McCarthy was forced to haul a corpse through two movies alongside Jonathan Silverman justifiably should have earned him a wealth of empathy from me.

The problem here is that–despite my general understanding that what happens on the silver screen is not real life–I'm having a difficult time separating my fictional emotions from my real ones. I'm fairly certain I don't hate Andrew McCarthy, but I know I hate Blane McDonough, and thus it is nearly impossible for me not to say to him exactly what is running through my head: *You didn't deserve her. You. Did. Not. Fucking. Deserve. Her.*

Fortunately for all parties involved, standing between Andrew and my scorn is the producer of the evening's show, who graciously introduces us to each other. Andrew shakes my hand and tells me that he is pleased to meet me, and I shake back and blubber out a string of sentences that likely indicate I've suffered a series of small strokes:

"I'm really excited to hear you perform my story. It's a real thrill for me to have you read this because, as a kid, I thought I was you for a time." *Did I just say that? I didn't think I was you. I thought I was Duckie. Wait. If I just said that (and I'm pretty sure that I did, because you're looking at me a little strangely and I can sort of feel you wanting to take your hand back from my grasp, which would be fine, except that I think I'm having a moment of absolute clarity here and I think you, Andrew McCarthy, Blane Fucking McDonough, are the conduit), then my entire life might be a lie. So let me just hold you for a moment more, Andrew.* "It's an important story for me because," I continue, "it really shows the interior depths that a child can go to."

I smile like nothing at all has happened, like I haven't just possibly made this nice gentleman a wee bit freaked out by my proclamation that we might have some sort of deeper emotional connection. It must be slightly disconcerting to be approached by a frumpy Jewish author who believes *he was you*, particularly on the evening you're about to read his work.

"It should be fun," Andrew says, and I release him from my grip. "We'll talk after and you can tell me what you think."

"Great! Yes. Fantastic!"

I slither my way back through the crowd to the table where my wife, Wendy, is sitting. She has a look on her face that I've come to associate with the ten or so most embarrassing moments of my life, which is to say the moments I've been away from her side and have, by no fault of hers, done some insanely stupid shit in her line of vision.

"How'd it go?" Wendy asks.

"Good. He was pleased to meet me."

"Did you say anything you're going to regret?"

"That I'm going to regret? No. That I currently regret? Possibly."

The problem with encountering people who made a large impression on you as a teenager, in the presence of a person who has known you only as an adult, is that you're apt to revert back to your teenage self. It's why I've pledged not to go to any more high school reunions and why, as of right now, I think that I'm going to pledge not to meet anyone else who starred in a John Hughes film. It's just too . . . personal.

You spend a good portion of your life figuring out who you are, either by virtue of intensive therapy or simple wretched personal experience, and then you eventually reach a point where you become comfortable in your skin, for better or worse or by direction of law enforcement officials. But when you're a teenager, the ability to see a time when life will be what you make it isn't always such an easy proposition, so you identify with what you find most appealing.

The 1980s weren't exactly my golden years, particularly since I didn't "graduate" out of special education until 1982, when I was eleven. Back in the '70s and early '80s the general wisdom was to stick kids with dyslexia into special-education classes alongside children with severe issues. There was Natalie, the girl with hooks for arms who liked to periodically pee on the floor. There was Darren, the boy in the wheelchair who liked to jerk off in class. And there was Sam, whom even Darren and Natalie called Spastic Sam, owing to the fact that he was profoundly crazy and liked to hit himself in the face with heavy objects.

All of which is a long way of saying that I felt like a freak and, because of my special-education background, kids around me typically treated me like one too. It didn't help that I was about fifty pounds overweight and had all the socialization skills of an aspiring serial killer.

The next few years were filled with trial and error as I tried to fit into different crowds, constantly attempting to reinvent myself based on what I thought was cool, which ended up being not all that cool. There was the Parachute-Pants-and-Ear-Clip Debacle, a life choice borrowed from the salesman at Merry-Go-Round who convinced me to spend all of my savings on sleeveless Chams shirts and bottles of Drakkar Noir cologne. There was the failed attempt at being Goth– an endeavor I embarked upon with my best friend, Todd–that was doomed by my fondness for Rick Springfield, my general lack of localized anguish (by this point I was already in therapy), and an allergy to pancake makeup. There was even a brief flirtation with being preppy that ended when I'd stained all of my preppy clothing and was thus forced back into the clutches of Goth, if only for the winter.

Nothing worked. People still called me a retard. By the time I was fourteen, I was pretty confident that my first sexual experience was going to come in prison, where I'd be sent after I murdered one of the various bullies who'd made my life torturous. In fact, I'd already started writing short stories where various classmates of mine met nasty ends (I recall death by impalement as a particular favorite), stories that now actually *would* land me in prison if I wrote them as a student.

That year, however, two things happened that changed me: My family and I moved, and I embraced the movies of John Hughes.

Moving was the key aspect of the equation. I decided that when I got to my new town–Palm Springs–I was going to create myself anew, but that this time there'd be no one there who knew about my special-ed past, and thus I could be whoever I wanted to be.

John Hughes made it easy: I could be Jake Ryan instead of Farmer Ted. I could be Andy Clark instead of Brian Johnson. I could be Claire Standish instead of Allison Reynolds. Hughes's movies proved that even the geekiest, most socially abnormal kids were, in fact, just as interesting and smart as the popular ones (and often had the same problems), irrespective of what the social Darwinism of the public school system had to say about the subject—but I'd already been a retard and preferred just to enter the social strata at the top, thank you very much.

Yes, I decided, I would be popular. I would listen to cool music, would wear cool clothes, would say cool things, and people would look at me and say, "Wow, that Tod Goldberg is *cool.*" I wouldn't read books in the quad. I wouldn't listen to Rick Springfield (or Neil Diamond). I wouldn't draw attention to myself in class by being any smarter than I needed to be. I would be Jake Fucking Ryan if it killed me.

I ended up as Duckie.

Jim, my oldest friend from high school, admitted to me recently that for the first two years of our friendship he was pretty certain I was gay or, possibly, a eunuch. I found this surprising, not least of all because I'm straight and have never been without my testicles.

"It was that stupid fedora and those thrift-store suits you'd wear to school," he said. "And how you followed all those girls around like a puppy dog and were into the Smiths and the Cure and pegged all your pants and wore those shoes with fur on them."

"Creepers," I said.

"What?"

"The shoes were called creepers and they were very cool."

"No they weren't," he said. "I was there. They were totally not cool."

"If it wasn't cool," I said, "why would John Hughes have dressed Duckie like that in *Pretty in Pink*?"

"Dude," Jim said, "they didn't work for Duckie, either. You picked the wrong guy to model yourself after."

Jim had hit on the very sad truth of my teenage existence: When faced with a choice of male role models, even when I knew better, I invariably gravitated toward the lovable loser.

At some point between deciding I'd be Jake Ryan and the onset of reality, I ended up vaguely resembling a member of the Pet Shop Boys, which meant I wore a lot of suits and spent a great deal of time frowning, two attributes that don't scream "Looking for macho companionship" apparently, and began allowing my sister Linda to color my hair and pick out my clothes. This seemed like a good idea at the time. It wasn't. When I finally realized the error of my ways, it was the middle of my freshman year, I had orange hair, and Linda had run away from home and was living in Los Angeles.

I recall, with vivid clarity, going to see *Pretty in Pink* with a big group of my friends—Tania, Lise, Kindy, Becky, Tawny, Michelle, and Denise, all of whom had boyfriends named Jason, Tyler, or Scott who looked like Jake Ryan—and finding a kindred spirit in Jon Cryer's Duckie. He had impeccable style. He had a great hat. He was lovable. He admired Otis Redding. He deserved to get the girl in the end (categorically *not* the girl he does get—the mythical blond woman who causes Duckie to break the fourth wall with a knowing smirk that seems to admit to the audience that none of this was meant to happen, that it was all rewritten and reshot to appease a test audience or an actor, or to satisfy a Faustian deal John Hughes entered into with Andrew McCarthy's agent). And he was secure in who he was.

That was me, right down to the fucking hat and minus all the positive attributes. I have photos to prove it. The problem is that women don't want to be romantic with someone they consider their shoulder. Eventually even the shoulder would break their heart, and then where would they turn? Other men are also not real keen on hanging out with their girlfriend's best friend, particularly if their girlfriend's best friend happens to be the weird new kid wearing a fucking wool suit in the middle of spring. After *Pretty in Pink* this was all pretty clear to Tania, Lise, Kindy, Becky, Tawny, Michelle, and Denise as well: I made the perfect love-worn sidekick. They even began to call me pet names like Tody, Todster, and Todler. I was about as sexy as a chew toy.

This was not a future I wanted. Hell, I don't think it was a future Jon Cryer wanted—a career of playing the roles Tony Randall got too old for, until, for all intents, he became Tony Randall—and neither of us wanted to be so nebulous sexually that people either thought we were gay or had missed a tremendous opportunity to be so. Not only did I want to eventually get the girl, as Duckie obviously did, I wanted to deserve her as well. If John Hughes ever made a misstep in his writing career (apart, obviously, from *Weird Science*), it was giving Molly Ringwald's Andie Walsh to Andrew McCarthy's Blane McDonough at the end of *Pretty in Pink*. He should have known better: In *Sixteen Candles* everyone, even Long Duk Dong, found their perfect somebody, the one person who would love them into celluloid forever. In *The Breakfast Club* everyone, even Anthony Michael Hall's überdork Brian, who fell in love with his own words, ended up in the arms of a person who could take them places emotionally or physically or through pawning the diamond earring they were given for a pack of smokes and the gumption to call child-protective services.

John Hughes established that the marginalized would find their margin, that those truly in love would not go about life in a fit of unrequited yearning, that if you were decent and capable of epiphany, you would be rewarded with your fondest hopes. Adult reasoning suggests that most of the relationships Hughes put in motion were actually destined for bone-crushing failure.

Just consider the statistical odds of these scenarios ever working out:

1. Jake Ryan and Samantha Baker in *Sixteen Candles*: Jake was college bound and was about ten minutes from the statutory rape of sixteen-year-old ingenue Samantha Baker.

2. Farmer Ted and Jake's girlfriend, Caroline, in *Sixteen Candles*: The geeky freshman had sex with the passed-out-drunk prom queen (not to mention that he had his buddies take photos of her) that may or may not have been consensual. We call that date rape these days. Or just rape. Whichever, Caroline should be happy MySpace didn't exist in the 1980s.

3. The couples in *The Breakfast Club*: They all faced the inevitable reality of Monday-morning homeroom. Like Bender was going to prom with Claire? Like Allison was going to start cheering for Andy at his wrestling matches?

Unfortunately, when I saw *Pretty in Pink*, I wasn't an adult, and thus I believed that by the end of the movie Andie would see that all she needed was Duckie and, by extension, that Tania, Lise, Kindy, Becky, Tawny, Michelle, and Denise would systematically begin fighting for my affections. Why, when Andie and Duckie entered the prom hand in hand, the strains of OMD's ode to breaking up with heart-crushing regret, "If You Leave," resounding like a Greek chorus, a vanquished James Spader to one side, a doe-eyed Andrew McCarthy to another, I simply figured that the credits were going to roll over the frozen visage of the two lovers on the screen and that someone's tongue would find its way into my mouth.

Duckie deserved Andie, and Blane deserved to drag a fucking corpse around through two movies alongside Jonathan Silverman. Metaphorically speaking.

That's how it had to work. It's what John Hughes promised. The rich and socially powerful never won. The retards were always victorious. But that didn't happen. And because that didn't happen, I didn't get Tania, Lise, Kindy, Becky, Tawny, Michelle, or Denise. I got a hat, a collection of Otis Redding albums, furry shoes, and an amorphous sexual identity for two years.

As drinks and appetizers are served, I try not to stare at Andrew McCarthy. I've written only one blatantly autobiographical short story–and by "autobiographical" I mean only that I've used bits and pieces of my life as inspiration for something larger, not a story that is strictly based on my own life–and it's the story Andrew McCarthy is about to read, as soon as he finishes his plate of bow-tie pasta. It follows a boy through a treacherous time in his life, filled with special-education classes, confused issues of sexuality, sudden violence, and Otis Redding. The story ends with the boy as a man, living a normal life, an outward success, but who still yearns for bits and pieces of who he once was.

Here I am, sitting with my wife, preparing to hear an actor read a story that is loosely based on a period of my life hallmarked by . . . him.

After realizing that being Duckie was a recipe for being a complete and total reject, I made some hard decisions about who I was, who I wanted to be, and who I was likely to become. The answer was that I wasn't anybody; I was just a compendium of influences that didn't amount to anything more than a personality disorder.

What's brilliant about high school is that you're given three months off every year to transform yourself. So that's what I did, but instead of aping some style or band or actor, I just came to the first day of school as me. I climbed the social ladder because I simply didn't give a fuck anymore, which is apparently very attractive to young men and women alike. And what I found was that being cool wasn't about forgetting your special-ed past or wearing clothes that made you look like the third Pet Shop Boy, or even about being particularly smart or the perception that you might be stupid. It was about having the confidence to be, simply. Just to be.

Or it didn't happen like that at all. It's hard to say for sure because it's now part of a different kind of mythology, a part of my past that I bring out to laugh at sometimes but that is also so painful that I think I've ascribed emotions to my teenage self that are really just the purview of a thirty-five-year-old man trying to reason with how his life has become so good when it came from such a weird place. Because that's how it would have ended in a John Hughes movie, a fantasy of how I wished my own life would be, sound track and all. Maybe I just grew up and stopped trying to eat myself alive.

It occurs to me, as I watch Andrew McCarthy make his way from his table, where he's been sitting beside his own wife, up to the raised stage at the front of the room, that I've hated the wrong guy all these years. No one deserves anybody.

Andrew McCarthy begins reading my story, and it sounds like how I always imagined it would sound, which isn't very descriptive, I know, but trust me when I say that he embodies a character that has lived inside me for as long as I've been able to conjure the feelings of loss and anger and sadness and joy that my childhood stained me with.

"He's phenomenal," Wendy whispers midway through the performance. "He really understands the character."

More so, I think, than he'll ever know.

Which John Hughes Character Are You?

by Nina de Gramont

About a year ago I took an Internet quiz called "Which John Hughes Character Are You?" I answered every question honestly, afraid that nearly twenty years after I'd graduated from high school–during which most of these movies premiered–I'd turn out to be the mom from *Sixteen Candles*, or worse, Harry Dean Stanton from *Pretty in Pink*.

The Web site tallied up my score and proclaimed me to be not Stanton's Jack Walsh at all, but his on-screen progeny: Andie Walsh. I was disdainful. The one scene I remembered from *Pretty in Pink* was where Andie–played by Molly Ringwald–shreds that perfectly pretty prom dress in order to make a hideous potato sack with bizarre cutout shoulders.

I was not, and had never been, Andie Walsh.

You'd think that would be that. But a few months later–for reasons of procrastination or insomnia–I took the quiz again. Not a true believer in the science of Internet quizzes, I assumed the results would be different this time, based on mood and whim. "Which John Hughes Character Are You?" With such myriad possibilities, the answer to that question could not be static, but subject to the changing vagaries of day-to-day life. That certainly would have been the case during my teenage years. Unpredictable and disobedient, I'd gone to three different high schools, embodying a different type at each one.

But apparently adulthood had rendered me more stable. After I'd answered every question (less thoughtfully, more automatic this time), the results were the same: "You are Andie Walsh," the Web site informed me. "Misunderstood and full of angst, you are intelligent, talented, and will probably go on to do great things . . . once you're out of the hell of high school." Below this pronouncement were the stats: "This quiz has been taken 16934 times. 22% of people had this result."

I decided there might be more science to this quiz than I'd previously thought.

I took it again, this time answering the eight questions as if I had not been out of the hell of high school lo these past twenty years. Probably being a little unkind to my teenage self, I chose the answers that most applied circa 1984. In response to the question "How adaptable are you to change?" I checked "I'm along for the ride, as long as things work out okay for ME!" (As my present-day incarnation I'd checked the box next to "Calm-headed—I can usually figure something out.")

The Web site performed its instantaneous tally and informed me that as a teenager I had been Buck Russell, from *Uncle Buck*, which I hadn't even realized was a John Hughes movie. "Your relationships aren't the greatest (mostly by your own accord)," I read, "but if anyone has a huge heart, it's you."

I stared at the computer screen, at the pop-up photo of John Candy's sweet, smiling face. Though not a big fan of ribald comedy, I'd always liked him. Just looking at him made me feel sad, and not just because of his early demise. Never mind that back in high school I'd rarely crested a hundred pounds; the idea that I had started life as Uncle Buck and grown up to be Andie Walsh made strange and startling sense.

• • •

"What is your financial status?"

Forget *Uncle Buck*. When we consider John Hughes, that's not the sort of film that comes to mind. Instead, think *The Breakfast Club*. Think *Sixteen Candles* and *Ferris Bueller's Day Off*. These are the movies that nobody my age can have escaped seeing, never mind whether we called ourselves fans. One way or another—on the big screen or on video—we saw the films and identified with the characters despite their occasional caricature. When "Don't You (Forget About Me)" comes on the radio, we are primally encoded to listen to at least a few bars.

Of course I had seen *Pretty in Pink*, but I couldn't remember much beyond the aforementioned dress shredding. So I rented a copy and watched it on my daughter's portable DVD player. My husband caught a few minutes of the movie from over my shoulder. "What kind of high school is this?" he demanded, referring to the division between the expensively but hideously dressed "richies" (driving convertible Beemers) and the equally hideously but more cheaply dressed friends of Andie Walsh. From a fashion perspective the movie instantly confirmed my suspicions. Molly Ringwald looks luminous and ravishing in her close-ups, but when the camera pulls back, she is dressed like a funky old lady on an art tour of Santa Fe.

Which might be very close to the way I appeared to the frighteningly fashionable students at my second high school. A private school in Riverdale, New York, nobody there had an out-of-work father like Harry Dean Stanton—but just living in a building without a doorman could constitute the wrong side of the tracks, never mind commuting from Englewood, New Jersey. Illustrious parents of my day included Jules Styne and Ivan Boesky. The year I entered as a sophomore, three girls in my class had their sweet-sixteen parties at Regine's. One of my classmates, Ali Gertz—the rich white girl who would famously put AIDS on the Upper East Side map—contracted the disease at sixteen from a bartender she'd met at Studio 54, not an uncommon hangout for my underage contemporaries.

In contrast, I was small, ill dressed, and unworldly, and looked much younger than my fifteen years. Not exactly a recipe for social success in this new and preposterously upscale world. At my previous school, which I'd attended since kindergarten, I'd been grandfathered into the popular crowd. When my parents transferred me in an attempt to curtail my increasingly wild behavior, I assumed I'd enjoy the same privileges at my new school. To this end, I glommed on to the one person I knew at the school who already belonged to the elite group of girls, an old friend from summer camp. As children, Victoria Gould and I had been close. But hard as I worked to capitalize on the association, she worked doubly hard to shed it. Embarrassed by my uncut hair and baggy corduroys, Victoria would roll her eyes and cross her arms in extravagant exasperation whenever I drew near. When I used her as an excuse to nonchalantly join her friends at their brutally exclusive lunch table, Victoria publicly accused me of sucking up to Ali Gertz, which I no doubt did, Ali being the only one of those girls who was ever nice to me (it is worth noting here that Molly Ringwald played Ali in the TV movie based on her life).Victoria's ridicule had its desired effect, and I retreated–tail between my legs–to the other side of the cafeteria.

(Victoria Gould recently had a business lunch with a dear friend of mine named Matthew Davis. Discovering the mutual acquaintance, Victoria told Matthew that she and I had been "best friends." Best friends, Victoria Gould? With best friends like you, who needs snotty high school girls?)

Of course, Andie Walsh would never resort to so vindictive an aside. How much better she would have handled those years, let alone their memories! I had a similar reaction to the one time I caught an episode of *Dawson's Creek*: The teenagers sound not just like adults, but adults who've had years of therapy.

"If somebody doesn't believe in me, I can't believe in them," Andie Walsh announces with unwavering certainty. If only her tools of insight and self-esteem had been available to me during those lonely and uncertain years. I could never have lectured my father on his emotional availability or career choices—I was too busy stealing five-dollar bills from his wallet. But Andie Walsh, sure of herself and her own perception of justice, could put adults on the road to self-awareness. In one day she could set her ne'er-do-well father straight and then go on to teach the school principal a clearly worded thing or two about justice and tolerance.

Watching Molly Ringwald's pretty, earnest face on my daughter's ten-inch television screen, I chided myself for ever being insulted by the association. I should be so lucky! The character of Andie Walsh has the kind of fortitude I not only lacked as a teenager, but still aspire to in middle age. Andie Walsh—strong enough to spurn the advances of that smarmy and evil but oh-so-popular James Spader—would never have stooped to suck up to Victoria Gould, or even Ali Gertz.

Following my rejection by the popular girls, I made my first Uncle Buck–like choice, one Andie Walsh would never have made, which was to befriend Emily—a brilliant, pot-smoking girl. Emily wore ripped jeans or Indian skirts and multiple silver earrings. She was very creative, an excellent mathematician, and a devoted friend; I've no doubt she's gone on to do incredible things. But at the time, under her tutelage, I fell into precisely the same sort of antics—and then some—that my parents had hoped to avoid by sending me to a new school.

Not that there weren't moments of redemption. I think Andie might have approved of my second choice. During the hours not spent with Emily, I followed my interests and the less choosy, more Duckie-esque route known as the theater crowd.

"If someone attractive was to hit on you, how would you most likely react?"

This may be unfair, but it seems to me in retrospect—and possibly did at the time—that the popular boys at school were kinder than the popular girls. Perhaps this stemmed from their popularity being rooted in athletics rather than looks and money. Or perhaps it was because I experienced them from an even greater distance than I did the girls. One of my more distinct memories is going to my locker while two girls from the popular crowd discussed something urgently personal. Their waists were slim, their hair and gold hoop earrings huge, and their butts huger in too-tight Calvins. Hearing someone approach, they looked up, concerned, and then seeing it was only me, continued with their conversation. I may have been similarly invisible to the popular boys, but in a less calculated way. In their varsity jackets, they seemed more oblivious to the hierarchy, not engineering and adhering to it so ruthlessly, just enjoying the glow as they sailed triumphantly down the halls.

Tony Mahoney was a tall and blue-eyed basketball player who distinguished himself off the court by an interest in the theater. The fall I worked props and served as an extra on *The Skin of our Teeth*, he played the night watchman—strolling gracefully across the stage, billy club thumping against his long legs. All the girls in the cast and crew adored him, but none of us had the courage to speak to him. So it was probably out of sheer loneliness that one day, while waiting in the wings, he asked me my name. I told him, then asked for his.

"Tony Mahoney," he said.

"That's very symmetrical," I said.

He smiled and said, "It's iambic."

Okay, so maybe the dialogue wasn't up to John Hughes. For actual high school it sufficed as witty repartee, enough to let us look at each other and laugh on a regular basis. A few days later, during a cast meeting, I found myself standing at the back of the stage next to Tony. As we listened to the director speak, Tony—with the casual air of a best friend's big brother—draped his arm across my shoulders. I froze, awestruck at the honor. The few girlfriends I had made in the theater world shot daggers in my direction (except for one sweet-faced beauty named Debbie, who gave me a thumbs-up).

The same spirit prevailed at the cast party, where Tony plopped himself down on the couch next to me. The next hour or two constituted my only happy experience associated with that school. Tony talked to me about his ideas, his love of beat poetry, the plays he had written.

The following Monday, I met Tony at his locker, where he gave me a copy of one of his plays. I kept it in my book bag all that day—its heat generating the promise that soon I would have a tall, handsome, and popular playwright as my boyfriend. Passing Victoria Gould in the hall, I bestowed a condescending and triumphant smile, certain that whatever charms she might hold for her wealthy and exclusive friends, Tony Mahoney would never give her Calvin-swathed butt a second glance.

That afternoon, riding the chartered bus home to New Jersey, I couldn't wait any longer and cracked open the pages of the play. I settled into the didactic and charmingly chaotic story of anarchy and mayhem. A few pages in, Diane—a senior from another high school—popped up over the seat in front of me. "What are you reading?" she asked.

I held up the script proudly, the illustrious words "by Tony Mahoney" emblazoned on the cover.

Diane laughed. The play, she told me, had been performed at the school last year. The entire auditorium had erupted in jeers. It was, she assured me, a humiliating farce.

I dived back into the script, worriedly reading the words Tony had written. Suddenly the creativity seemed stale, the ideas silly. Although I didn't provide Diane—casting occasional and expectant looks back at me—with the derision she clearly requested, neither did I come to Tony's defense.

And neither did I allow Tony's interest in me to continue. It didn't take much to discourage him—he, after all, was the one making a social leap downward. One glance in the other direction as he came toward me down the hall, and there went Tony Mahoney, off to date a beautiful and devastatingly cool blonde just back from a semester in Paris. I realized my gigantic mistake too late and, even when they broke up, never managed to achieve much more than a return glance and vague nod from the guy who should have been my Andrew McCarthyesque prom date, if only I'd been as sure of myself as Andie Walsh, and my high school provincial enough to have a prom.

Looking back at these events for the first time in many years—re-creating my own skewed and probably faulty version—I'm impressed by Tony's ability, as a teenager, to channel his inner Blane McDonough and express an interest in someone like me. I'm impressed by his ability to have withstood schoolwide ridicule, assuming what Diane said was even true, and still present his script proudly to an indoctrinated reader.

Equally I'm unimpressed by my own inability to do either of the same, even when it would have meant a stratospheric leap in social status. The ridicule that he'd received, endured, and dismissed was too much for me, even by association. I remained boyfriendless (and pining for Tony) until I left that high school for Putney—a boarding school where the groovy clothes Emily had taught me to wear served my social standing well.

"Finally, which words do you think best fit your personality? (Choose all that apply.)"

There's something to it, the dichotomy of childlike personalities in adult life and adult personalities in high school. The appeal of Uncle Buck to teenagers is clear–the delight in seeing an adult who's managed to escape the responsibility most of them face with trepidation. And to adults, a sort of vicarious fulfillment, along with the vindication of seeing Uncle Buck finally admit that family and steady income are the only road to true happiness.

The last question on the "Which John Hughes Character Are You?" quiz listed eighteen adjectives: "boisterous," "serious," "silly," "magnetic," "businesslike," "charming," "caring," "anxious," "impatient," "intelligent," "emotional," "persuasive," "optimistic," "exuberant," "childish," "family-oriented," "coolheaded," "happy-go-lucky." As an adult, I checked off these words to apply to myself: "serious," "caring," "anxious," "intelligent," "emotional," and "family-oriented."

If I had answered the questions for myself as a teenager honestly–not as myself looking back at me, but as I would have answered them at the time–I probably would have checked off every single adjective except for "family-oriented" and "businesslike." Certainly I desperately wanted to be charming and magnetic, optimistic and exuberant. And maybe–in some youthful and searching way–I was.

But never in the self-examining way endemic to certain characters in films about youth. Something about watching *Pretty in Pink* reminded me of that dream we all have, the one where, through some strange and inexplicable series of events, we are our own grown-up selves returned to high school. Only this time, instead of being too old to fit in with the kids, we inhabit the shiny bodies of our past and the reasoned intellects of our present. We appreciate the return to our unlined faces and taut skin, and the endless possibilities waiting for us off in the adulthood that seems as fictional and unknown as the end of a rainbow.

As for the ruthless social politics, the gossiping teenage girls: We understand that this, too, shall pass. Watching the dynamics from both vantage points, we can navigate the brutal world with compassion and self-awareness. We can even find a way to make it all work.

Of course, that's not the way it ever happens while I'm sleeping. But peering into the tiny, DVD-fueled screen—remembering the eighties clothes, the cars, and more important, the timeless torture of high school—I get to see Andie Walsh do exactly that. It's not as good as getting that prom date for myself.

But it does come close.

La Vie en Rose

PRETTY IN PINK

by Tara Ison

It's 1986. The *Challenger* has exploded, and Chernobyl is about to burn. U.S. air strikes against Libya loom, and the World Court will declare the United States has violated international law by aiding the Nicaraguan contras. A terrorist bomb will blow up a TWA plane en route to Athens from Rome. Ultraconservative U.S. surgeon general C. Everett Koop will want children taught about anal sex as a defense against AIDS. A toxic gas eruption will float a lethal cloud over Cameroon. I am abruptly twenty-two years old, and everywhere I turn: radiation, lies, viruses, a shower of burning debris. I will graduate from college soon, and I have no clue what comes next. The "out there" of real life is only just beginning, but I have no plan. It's still early in 1986, and all I can do right now, it seems, is kill time. Just wait.

I will spend a lot of this year at the movies. I will go Wednesday and Friday afternoons to catch opening-day discount matinees. I will go every Saturday night and make a meal of a large salted popcorn and deep drinking-fountain slurps. I will go to retro, worn-velvet theaters to see revival noir, and to the multiplex for action adventures on postage-stamp screens. I will see everything. It's the year of *Top Gun* and *Platoon* and *Aliens*, and I will spend a lot of my time immersed in these visions of bombs and blood and evil, insinuating entities.

• • •

In late March of 1986 I go to see the latest John Hughes movie, *Pretty in Pink*. Why not? It's playing. *The Breakfast Club* was fun. *Sixteen Candles* was cute. I've always been a sucker for teen angst with attractive casting and good production design. And that Molly Ringwald is adorable. And it will fill two hours on this day. So I go. But I'm twenty-two now, too old for this kind of movie. I'm weary enough to see through it all. The archetypal high school love story–wrong-side-of-the-tracks girl loves handsome preppy boy–feels less archetypal than just plain precious and contrived. I'm old enough to see that preppy Andrew McCarthy/Blane is a spineless, impotent creep–not even a major appliance, a mere kitchen gadget–who is more pretty than handsome, even prettier, perhaps, than adorable Molly herself. I'm old enough to see that "quirky" best friend character Duckie is gay. That Molly Ringwald/Andie's self-made and sack-like pink prom getup–despite Duckie's insistence on "stunning"–is hideous. That the Andie and Blane love story we're supposed to root for and care about is bland and thin, grounded in nothing of substance, and wholly lacking any teenage heat or yearn. That slovenly but sweet Dad character is really a raging alcoholic who has abdicated his parental responsibility, that Andie's mom probably fled the house seven years earlier to escape his addiction and abuse, and that Andie's cool after-school job at the too-cool record store Trax isn't just paying for her vintage bits of leather and lace, it's probably paying for Dad's cooler of beer. That all the high schoolers–with the exception of sweet Molly–are far too old for their roles. That the only character in this movie worth fucking is oily Steff (James Spader). And wry and acerbic Iona (Annie Potts). And bit player Gina Gershon, of course, with whom I went to junior high school and who was pretty damn hot even then. It's all a big lie. This high school, these places and scenarios, these characters, these clothes, these relationships, never did and never could exist in the real world.

But I love this movie. I love this movie the second it begins—the moment the Psychedelic Furs hit the refrain on their watered-down version of "Pretty in Pink," my cynicism melts, dissolves, floats out of my body, and leaves space for a giddy happiness. I love the opening shots of Andie girding for battle, pulling on a pair of creamy opaque stockings to set off her thrift-store boots, bringing out the determination in those big brown eyes with a few mascara dabs. I love her thick red helmet of a bob, that breastplate vest of lace. She is a dewy-skinned, spunky Amazon with a pink phone and cleverly mismatched accessories. Her room is a dream teen fortress, artfully bannered with ribbons and scarves. I love how she's effortlessly smarter than everyone, how her intrinsic value as a person of quality, intelligence, and integrity is a powerful, unstoppable force, how she outshines the shallow, feather-haired, cleavaged girls, even to their own bitchy and begrudging eyes. I love that her best friend is the wry and acerbic and twice-her-age Iona, who is always on call to dispense maternal affection and wry, acerbic advice, and goes with her to cool clubs to drink sodas through straws and hear cutting-edge bands. I love dear Blane's delicate sensibility, and the chaste innocence of his and Andie's trysts, the unthreatening texture of their intimacy. I love how Andie sees such potential in him—and of course if she sees it, it is there—and how he will evolve thanks to her faith; I love how Andie becomes prettier when seen through his own pretty eyes. I love Duckie's painful worship of Andie—his lip-synched "Try a Little Tenderness" is a brilliant, resonant poem. I love her careful tending of her loving and befuddled father, how they work through their issues in a single scene that sets him back on a path to functional fatherhood. I love how Andie comes away a winner in the end, of course: The rich, sensitive boyfriend comes crawling back; the loyal, devoted buddy stands by her; she earns respect from the entire world; she has won both the battle and the war.

Yes, Andie's teen girlhood was my own—finally, on-screen, *me*! This was my own heartfelt and idiosyncratic high school dance. It is so real, so true to life. I was one of the quirky, too-bright over-achievers who eschewed the slick and shallow popular cliques. I wore Victorian petticoat bloomers to school and cut up my grandparents' curtains to make blouses and was an arbiter of singular style. I had a brilliant and artistic Duckie-like best friend (gay too) who made me feel like a rarified creature of note. And I did go out with the popular, prettier-than-me boy. I did get him to recognize my intrinsic value as a young woman of intelligence and honesty and integrity. Oh yes, I was Andie and Andie was me, and how delightful to revisit those halcyon, pretty-in-pink days.

Or no. Not quite. I'm twenty-two and old enough now, suddenly, abruptly, to be nostalgic for a version of a childhood and teen girlhood that never existed. I'm longing for a revision of my reality. I want a total remake. These days I am craving a *Room 222* earnestness, a *Happy Days* simplicity, a Gidget and Moondoggie kind of frivolous fun. Right now I am desperate to go back, look back, and identify with the artifice of this film. It isn't so much that the movie is a lie—it's that my own teenhood was a contrivance, a fake. A bad, overacted dress rehearsal performance by an unskilled understudy. The high school Andie of this movie is who I *wanted* to be, tried to be. I was never the cheerleader type or the Gina Gershon hot one or a fearless New Waver or punk; I was, yes, one of the "quirky, too-bright overachievers," but only by default—that was the clique elastic enough in definition and demographic to let me squeeze in. And I was just a minor and generic bit player, never a leading lady, never quite quirky or freakish enough to be referred to as "mutant" or shine out as a genuine outcast. I tried so hard. I told myself any social eschewing was by my choice. I got good enough grades to be a "smart girl," to get teachers to hawk my potential. But my piecemeal thrift-shop outfits looked foolish and forced—no "volcanic ensembles" for me. A bad perm and handfuls of mousse couldn't spunk up my defeated hair. My after-school job was thirty hours a week in a bakery/deli; I smelled like onions and got discounts on éclairs and potato salad, not funky albums to lure in dates or friends. Sure, my sweet dad was an alcoholic too, but there were punched-out holes in our walls. After my parents split up, my mother disappeared into a postdivorce second adolescence of her own, taking me with her to seedy bars to entice guys—no insightful heart-to-hearts or maternal advice to be had there. And my prize, my kind and pretty gold-star boyfriend of four months, did dump me prior to the prom—but I believe for him it was no brief stumble on his path toward appreciating me, it was just a wearying of my intrinsic, idiosyncratic value, exacerbated, I fear, by my refusal to allow him to get his hands down my pants or across my flat, flat chest.

But still, there is an honest point of connection here, a real thing to which I can relate: the theme of Andie's eventual escape from the limitations of her environment. She'll be appreciated, more and truly, once she's older. After Andie talks back to a gym teacher (off-screen, of course—we don't really want to see her as rebel smart-ass), the kindly principal diplomatically reminds her of her future, of her promise and potential. There is the suggestion she has already outgrown high school, is too mature and evolved to squander herself on these petty teenage snafus. We know her full beauty has yet to flower. Duckie might be flunking classes in order to stay in high school and not face the future, as Andie points out to him, but she is chomping at the bit. Scholarships and college and career await this powerful young girl with the no-nonsense brown eyes and the quivering Gothic-arch upper lip. *Life* awaits her, right *out there*. Just think what she'll achieve, what she'll be. She just has to graduate.

She will have it all. She's just warming up. I want to think that too. I have been told my whole life that I have promise and potential. I have just been biding my time. Everything is about the future—what I will achieve once, once, once. *Once* I am really out on my own, out of college, an adult. *Once* my uniqueness has room to bloom. *Once* everything falls into place, *once* real life begins. Just you wait.

But back up a bit. It's still earlier in 1986, February 1 to be exact, and I've been twenty-two for eight days. I miss being twenty-one, the "bridge" year, the year spent getting excited by, then slowly used to, the legal buying of booze. I go to see *Down and Out in Beverly Hills* with my best friend—the brilliant, artistic, gay one. It's opening night, we're waiting in line, eating M&M'S and playing word games. This is where I am right now, as an adult: M&M'S for dinner, and word games and Friday-night dates with my platonic buddy. I should be feeling further along, I think; I have my first real, ratty apartment, all on my own; my first grown-up job as personal assistant to an elderly, once-famous screenwriter; I am in the middle of my first serious, mature love throes with a guy who wants to keep me dangled and tangential at best. But my friend and I are still confused by our adult lives, still shamefully bewildered by the cipher of lease documents and checking account paperwork and tax forms, still clumsy at negotiating condoms and love. Wait, are we here yet, *are* we adults? No, *once, once*, we are still reassuring ourselves. Any day now. Once we graduate, of course. Just wait—how fabulous we will be, how successful and secure. How much promise and potential we have. Something will happen, it has to. Adulthood threatens like the nuclear bombs we spent our childhood expecting to hit, to suddenly fly through our school windows, shattering then melting the glass. Drop and cover, we were taught. This is what I really want to do now, drop and cover and hide from my looming (no, it's here, actually, wake up) adulthood, but I have outgrown my childhood desk.

Even worse, however–I am starting to suspect that my "promise and potential" is just a line told to any mildly quirky, mildly over-achieving kid, an encouraging pleasantry. I am starting to fear there is yet another clique far beyond my grasp, the clique of gracefully successful, achieving, nononiony adults. A very private club with cinder-block, barbed-wire-topped walls; with guarded, padlocked gates; and a membership exam so exquisitely obtuse as to be incomprehensible and unconquerable. I am starting to fear I am losing the battle, that I am waiting for the appearance and manifestation of nothing at all.

The theater line begins to move; I am happy that all that awaits me at the moment is a benign-looking Paul Mazursky comedy. We creep forward, crumpling our candy wrappings, and the world suddenly sweeps off to a thick-curtained blackness. I stumble into a void. Light and sound are snuffed out. When I open my eyes a blink later, I'm lying on the carpeted multiplex ground, my head in my best friend's lap and a ring of concerned strangers' faces overhead. Someone is clutching my foot. Someone is holding a wallet with drool on it. My best friend is wiping my chin. A seizure has carried me off; a small cerebral bomb has exploded, wiped out half an hour or so of my self. I have been briefly shattered. An ambulance, a gurney, a blurry ride to a hospital bed. Intake questions and forms. There is no family history of epilepsy. No personal history of neurological mishap. This is all quite a surprise, in fact. Clearly something is amiss. Clearly something has happened. Tubes and tests and scans. But it's a weekend; we have to wait until the real doctors come on Monday. There are a few days of mystery and excitement, of playing with hospital gown fashion, of sterile smells mingling with the delicious reek of fast food brought in by family and friends. All my limbs feel sore. We have no clue what's wrong with me; I just wait.

There is a team assembled: a neurologist; a radiologist; the primary care doctor I have seen only once in my life, having graduated still recently, it feels, from the pastels and stuffed bears of pediatrics. There it is, they say: a lump. A tumor. A pinto-bean-size mass. My brain's left frontal lobe is housing an alien, insinuating thing, a burning bit of debris, a tiny toxic cloud. Radiation looms.

For the first time in my life I feel very, very adult. The Rubicon has been crossed. The demarcation line is clear. I have graduated, indeed, at last.

And this is, initially, wonderful to me. Talk about promise and potential! There is an opportunity here for drama. For big-screen heroics. Or stardom in a television movie of the week, at least. A young woman, a beautiful life just begun, stricken by a brain tumor! How brave our spunky young heroine is, how strong! How tragic! Finally, a clear role to play! Finally, an engraved invitation to a very exclusive club! Finally, a path, a plan!

Fortunately, I belong to a famously cheap and cost-cutting HMO–there will be no racing off to brain surgery, no leaping into costly treatments or cures. No wrapping this up, one way or another. Let's take it slow. Let's just monitor the tumor, see how it grows, how it manifests. Yes, by all means, let's drag this out. It'll give me something to do. Let's just wait.

Antiseizure meds thicken and coat your mind; it feels like Pepto-Bismol for your brain. I am nodding off in what is supposed to be my last round of college classes. I can't read beyond a paragraph without numbing out, and so I take a leave from school–I'll finish college at some point. Once everything is back to normal. I quit my neat new job. The guy I'm insane over, who was briefly reengaged by the dangled, tragic thrill, dumps me for good. I break the year lease on my first apartment, losing the deposit, and I move in with my grandfather. I sleep on his velveteen couch, the way I used to as a little girl, and drink root beer floats with him for breakfast. I'm not allowed to drive; I am advised not to shower when alone in the house. I am now, paradoxically, an infantilized adult. I have no idea what comes next, what awaits. I go to and from the hospital for repeated tubes and tests and scans. Every few weeks the medical team decides it's time to just go on in, let's cut the thing out, whatever it is, and I ready myself to shave off my limp, defeated hair. But the tumor doesn't seem to be growing. It's just hanging out, waiting for something to happen. The team schedules surgeries, then cancels them. Let's keep waiting. I'm sluggish and doped up. It's still early in 1986, and all I can do right now, it seems, is kill time. Just wait.

This will go on for many, many, many months.

Is this *the action and adventure of adulthood?* I finally start to wonder. *Or is this just more stalling?*

I will spend a lot of this year at the movies.

So I sit, at twenty-two, and watch *Pretty in Pink.* "You're gonna OD on nostalgia," Andie says to Iona, who is looking back to her own halcyon, floating-chiffon prom days, and I am too. I'm dying to. I'm dreamily swaying along with Iona to "Cherish," I'm eating it all up. I am loving every one of Andie's trials and tribulations, every victory, every smart comeback, every hairstyle, every singular outfit she's put together, every winsome bite of her lip and effortless scrap of lace. Every time Blane gives her one of his darling, insecure smiles, or Duckie proffers his adoration, I feel so pretty, so pink. Right now I need this. Watching this movie, I get to back up a few years and linger a moment in the chiffon fantasy of promise and potential. I get to recast all the roles, rewrite the dialogue, get the lip gloss on straight. I get to look back, vicariously and through rose-colored glasses, and this is much, much better, at this exact moment in life, than trying to look ahead.

Pretty in Pink was a huge hit in 1986; midyear *Time* magazine took a break from the "out there" of real life to put Molly on the cover—AIN'T SHE SWEET? they asked. I read on a slew of websites that John Hughes apparently wanted Molly Ringwald to star in his next film the following year, an archetypal wrong-side-of-the-tracks boy loves pretty preppy girl love story, but she declined—"You can't be sixteen forever," she said. True, but you were once, sweet Molly, and eternally; it's now 2006, and I hear the upcoming DVD rerelease of *Pretty in Pink* will have the original ending—Andie winds up with Duckie—and lots of new commentary. I'm looking forward to that. There are also rumors of a *Pretty in Pink* sequel—Andie, Blane, and Duckie twenty years later. They will all be adults. There will be inflated-rate mortgages and spirit-crushing jobs, romantic and familial trials and tribulations, disillusionments and grown-up angst. Bouts of despair, bouts of illness, and bad fright that eventually resolved just fine. Or didn't. Perhaps even wasted potential or unfulfilled promise. But they will all look fabulous, they will be sweet and smart and intelligent and ultimately victorious over it all. There will be a fabulous sound track and great production design, and, despite my cynicism, I will allow myself, for a ten-dollar ticket, to take a giddy two-hour break, to drop and cover from real life and all the present-day crashings and bombings and viruses and lies. I'll be in the front row, at an opening-day matinee, a large tub of popcorn in my lap. I can't wait.

Ferris Bueller

AN INFATUATION, A LIFE LESSON, AND ONE HARMLESS FAMILY ADVENTURE

by Allison Lynn

When I pick up the phone, my mother's a wreck on the other end. Either someone's died, I figure, or her book group has assigned another doozy. She's still in recovery from the Orhan Pamuk fiasco, when all thirty club members flailed through *My Name Is Red*. As it happens, today's problem involves neither fatalities nor abstruse fiction.

My youngest sister has turned up at Boston's South Station, alone.

"No way," I say. My sister may be well into her twenties, but she has significant learning disabilities, problems that frequently turn everyday life into a frustrating ordeal. She has the math skills of a third grader, and when she gets nervous, the mere act of adding one-digit numbers can stymie her. She blushes easily. She often awkwardly hugs people when she's supposed to shake their hand. She's charming and naive and, given the serious trouble she has grasping abstract concepts, sees the world in black and white. She also has no ATM card, almost no cash to her name this week (she's being taught how to live on a budget), and no car, or even a driver's license yet. It's astounding that she made it out of her hometown in the Berkshires—her home is a loosely supervised apartment, an exercise in interdependent living—let alone three hours east to South Station.

What happened? As my mother tells it, over the past twelve hours my sister Sarah has traveled through Cape Cod, Rhode Island, and Boston, all by bus and all in search of a no-good ex-boyfriend who promised to take her out if she could get to his hometown bus station in eastern Massachusetts. This particular cad is not real good when it comes to keeping promises. And Sarah's not real good at navigating the world alone. Still, she made it through a number of the Northeast's major travel hubs before she found herself, hours after dark, stood up and out of bus tickets—and stuck. Meanwhile, we, the people closest to her, had no idea she'd gone anywhere at all. We were as oblivious as Ferris Bueller's parents on the day he skips school, steals a car, ascends the Sears Tower, joins a parade, and teaches his best friend how to live.

"I'm so proud of her," I tell my mother, about my sister. In fact, I couldn't be prouder.

"She could have been killed," my mom responds, her voice shaking on the other end of the phone.

Matthew Broderick was my first love. I fell for him and I fell hard. I'd previously proved immune to celebrity crushes. I sat out the entire Shaun Cassidy era, and while the bulk of my fifth-grade friends were swooning over Leif Garrett, the slightest glimpse of his Farrah flip made me want to puke. And not the good kind of puke, the ohmigod-he's-dreamy puke. The dude made me feel genuinely ill.

Matthew Broderick was different. The movie that launched my fixation was *WarGames*, in 1983, the summer before my first year of high school. I was fresh off the eighth-grade graduation party season, when I had assumed I'd land my first kiss, but didn't. What was I looking for in a man back then, when I was thirteen? Anyone I could get. And in *WarGames*, Matthew Broderick seemed nothing if not attainable. He plays a high school computer geek who hacks into a Defense Department computer and then does the right thing by trying to save the world.

I had a computer back then, and though I never hacked into anything more secure than a box of Frosted Flakes, I was quite proficient at Olympic Decathlon and not bad at Asteroids. And I'd known for years already that tic-tac-toe was ultimately unwinnable. So Matthew and I had a lot in common. And unlike the members of the Shaun Cassidy/Leif Garrett posse, Broderick was no looker. Lookers, I'd learned from experience, were tough to nab. Sure, at the end of *WarGames*, Broderick gets the girl (Ally Sheedy, who sprouted three new inches of leg for the role), but not because he's handsome and cool. He's neither. Ally Sheedy loves him for his smarts. She is attracted to his mind rather than his debonair moves or his prime spot on the lacrosse team or his access to his parents' liquor cabinet. Trust me, I'd already made plays for plenty of guys who had French relatives and lacrosse sticks and Smirnoff at their disposal, and none of them had fallen for thirteen-year-old me. A smart nerd like Broderick, though—these kinds of guys were ripe for the picking, and I didn't think I'd have much competition.

John Hughes and his take on growing up in the suburban heartland wouldn't hit theaters until the following year, when *Sixteen Candles* debuted. Hughes would eventually teach me that it was okay to be myself. He'd insist that the jocks and prom queens weren't the only cool kids on the block—and that if I wanted to date one of those jocks anyway, they weren't, truly, out of my reach. But in 1983, before Hughes and his ethos hit big, it was just me and Matthew Broderick (and maybe Ally Sheedy, if she wanted to be our third wheel) against the much cooler and hipper world.

· · ·

Men don't change: This is the firm maxim I picked up, as a teen, from listening to talk radio in the car with my mother. "You get what you pay for!" the on-air docs cautioned an endless stream of callers, mostly women who'd chosen to date drunks or marry cheaters. Yet, on the surface, Matthew Broderick changed right before my eyes. Three years after his stunning, crush-inducing turn as a techno-nerd in *WarGames*, he arrived in style as Ferris Bueller. Ferris had a hot girlfriend and Brit-pop posters on the walls of his room and was envied by his peers. He owned a beret. Broderick, the outsider actor, the guy who played characters who'd never be cool in a real high school, had become the king of the insiders.

I see now that it wasn't, truly, the actor who'd changed. It was teen movies. They'd morphed in the mid-1980s. During these central Hughes years the stock stud characters, jocks and surfers, lost their lock on the romantic leading roles. The nerds and smart alecks and Matthew Brodericks of Hollywood began to hold their own. Unlike in *WarGames*, where the nerd hero was an outsider at school, the nerds in Hughes's movies had the potential to be legitimately cool. Hughes cast Ferris as a hipster when the kid should have been nothing but a world-class geek. He rigs up a scientific pulley system to fool his parents into thinking he's home sick in bed. He preprograms his electronic keyboard, hacks into the school computer, and knows the words to "Danke Schoen," a song so dorky that Wayne Newton covered it. Ferris should be a loser, but Hughes elevates him to high school royalty. Ferris is cool *because* of these geek qualities, because he carries them off with pride, because he revels in them.

If most of John Hughes's teen comedies from the '80s are about lunchroom hierarchies and unrequited crushes and the inner beauty of the outsider, *Ferris Bueller's Day Off* carves out its own niche as the movie that isn't centered around romance or cliques. Ferris

Bueller can get any girl he wants, and everyone in the film is on equal clique standing with him. No one's a loser to Ferris, or to Hughes, except for the adults. Ferris even gives face time—well, voice time—to the prepubescent freshmen. He actually knows their names! *Ferris Bueller's Day Off* is instead about what happens beyond high school; it looks forward to the real world, where if you don't stop to smell the roses, you're missing out.

Hughes was obvious in bridging the teen-adult gap on screen. Though the extras in the movie were all real high schoolers of high school age, Broderick was deep into his twenties when the movie was filmed, and Alan Ruck, who plays best friend and fellow high school senior Cameron Frye, turned thirty just three weeks after the movie's release. Broderick and Ruck were adults, and they look it— the way they tower over the extras is like a wink-wink joke to the viewer. The basic *Ferris Bueller* storyline, too, speaks to both kids and grown-ups. People of all ages love to manipulate the machine for their own benefit; this is a natural human inclination. It's why your neighbors are stealing your Wi-Fi and cable access. It's why shoppers pilfer bin food at the grocery store and eat it before they get to the checkout aisle. They're convinced that they can get away with it. It's why certain wars get started, but that's another story.

Ferris Bueller's Day Off is, at its heart, a saga about this basic instinct and one fearless man-child willing to push it past his own personal limit. What separates Ferris from the average getting-away-with-it criminal (or politician) is that at the end of his exploits no one's been hurt. It's simply about the adventure, with a little lesson for his friend Cameron thrown in. Even Ferris's bitter sister picks up on the "Live free" moral by the time the day's over, and makes out with the sort of hellion (hello, Charlie Sheen!) that her gut has spent years warning her to steer clear of.

When I first saw *Ferris Bueller*, soon after it premiered, I felt bad for myself, and not just because Matthew Broderick had grown so cool that he was no longer a candidate for my dance card. I felt bad *about* myself. The character I most resembled from the movie was Ferris's sister–in her pre-Sheen incarnation–the whistle-blower and naysayer and toe-the-line tightwad. I was the kind of kid who'd never fake an illness or skip school. The few times I'd misbehaved and sneaked out of the house after curfew, I'd always left a note on my pillow: "Dear Mom and Dad, I have not been abducted. I am alive and in the driveway. Look out the window." Yes, I was so scared of getting caught that I never made it farther than my own back door. My friends, if they wanted to see me at 2 a.m., had to come to my place, with a pizza and a six-pack, to party on the asphalt just ten feet below my own bedroom window, mercifully on the opposite end of the house from where my parents slept.

Was this any way to go through life? In the words of Cameron Frye, "I realized it was ridiculous, being afraid, worrying about everything . . . all that shit. I'm tired of it."

But I was already too stubborn to change. My one hope was for my youngest sister–that despite all of the ways that the world was conspiring against her, she might grow up to show some of the gumption I lacked.

What do families of children with disabilities want for their kids? They want them to enjoy, to some degree, the same things that all children (and later, adults) enjoy. I wanted for Sarah to engage in some form of age-appropriate behavior, to show signs that she was reaping life's benefits–and even manipulating them–in the same ways that her peers were. We all knew that she wanted to go to Cape Cod to meet her good-for-nothing ex, but it never occurred to us that she'd be sneaky enough, and age-appropriate enough, to do it behind our backs.

I'd seen Sarah a week earlier. She'd come to New York in a chaperoned van full of friends to see *The Lion King* on Broadway–my parents had paid for her ticket and transportation months earlier–and before the play I took her out for pizza in the theater district. She was sullen and silent, lacking her usual ability to put an optimistic spin on things. When I asked her what was wrong, she very seriously explained that she needed to borrow $60.

I knew she was on a budget. Her financial coach up in the Berkshires was working to help her understand money. Although she can easily oil-paint a jazzy landscape and remember every detail of the spring vacation she took ten years ago, she still, in her twenties, has trouble counting out change and grocery shopping for herself. I wasn't supposed to supplement her meager weekly take, but she wouldn't have asked for $60 if it weren't urgent. I didn't want the girl to starve just because she'd blown her whole budget at the beginning of the week.

"What do you need sixty dollars for?" I asked.

"A bus ticket," she said. And then, as if I should be proud of her, she explained that she'd done the research herself and discovered that she could get a bus from the Berkshires to Boston and then switch to a bus to the Cape, and round-trip it would cost her only $60. After a long pause she added, "I've already asked my friends; they don't have any money to give me, so it's up to you."

"Did you ask Mom and Dad?"

Her face fell, fast, down the slippery slope from hope to shame. "They don't want me to go."

She hadn't mentioned the ex-boyfriend's name, but he was the only draw for her out there in eastern Mass., the only thing she'd blow sixty bucks of her own money for. We'd all warned her against him. Yet, again and again and again she'd let him draw her in close, only to stomp on her heart. When it comes to replacing her cell phone's battery, she eagerly asks for help from friends, from counselors, from family. Sarah knows she's not always equipped to handle that kind of transaction on her own. But when it comes to men, she's convinced that she's savvier than the rest of us. She thinks that people are easy to understand. She takes them at their face value and is constantly baffled when they prove to be more complicated, or more sinister, underneath. You can tell her this, you can remind her of when she's been wrong before, you can point out the mistakes she's made with other boys ever since she started dating, but it's no use. In the area of love it's proved impossible to protect her. Denying her the $60, though, seemed to be, finally, a foolproof way to keep her from making yet another mistake.

"So you're not going to give me the money?" she said, refusing to eat her pizza. I'd ruined her New York trip. Seeing *The Lion King* had clearly been just an excuse to come to the city and bilk me out of my cash. And it hadn't worked. "I have to go to the Cape."

"Men don't change, Sarah," is what I told her. "Give up on this guy."

I sat at a table next to Matthew Broderick a few years ago at a roadside clam shack in Amagansett, on the eastern tip of Long Island. I hadn't thought about him in at least a decade. He'd turned into a song-and-dance guy, hamming it up with Nathan Lane on Broadway. He'd married Sarah Jessica Parker, proving that I'd been wrong twenty years earlier when I estimated that he was the kind of man I'd be able to get for myself. He and his A-list wife lived just a few blocks away from me in the city, in an apartment with bathrooms the size of my entire pad.

It was a steamy day at the clam shack, and fry oil rose straight up from the paper baskets full of calamari and fish that sat on each table. Matthew and Sarah J. were eating with friends, shading their eyes from the sun and picking at their golden, crisp food. He wore all white. A white tee, white knee-length shorts, pale skin poking out underneath. Even in his snowy duds he looked as if he might sweat to death. Death by melting. We were all feeling that way.

"Did you see who that was?" asked one of my friends from across our table after the stars got up to leave.

"I used to have a mad crush on him," I said. All of the heads at my table turned around to get one last look before the Broderick-Parker crew drove away.

"I know. Ferris Bueller," all the women at the table swooned at once.

I talk to my sister Sarah the morning after her bus escapade. Here's her version of her personal Day Off:

Without my help, she scrounged up bus money, rode to Boston, and seamlessly transferred to a bus to the Cape, where she got off at the stop designated by her wayward paramour. The notorious louse didn't pick her up as promised. She waited for a while and then, dejected, got out her return ticket. When a bus arrived and was headed westward, she asked the other people who were boarding whether this was the coach to Boston. None of them would answer, she tells me. None seemed eager to talk to a stranger, especially one whose speech is sometimes tough to understand and who was probably nervous enough to be shaking a little and talking too quietly. Sarah boarded the bus anyway, last minute, before it could leave without her. It was headed to Providence.

Once in Providence, she determined that she still needed to get to Boston in order to finally make her way home to the Berkshires, but she didn't have enough money for the extra ticket and wasn't going to use her emergency escape route—my parents' credit card—since that was a sure way to get caught. She started to panic at the ticket window. A rude clerk told her that the last bus to Boston was about to leave, and if she didn't have the fare, she'd have to spend the night in Providence. Sarah had never booked a hotel room on her own, had never stayed anywhere solo, and knew not a soul in Rhode Island. And her cell phone was on the fritz. She began to wail, imagining a night spent alone on the street, and that's when, she says, the first of her "angels" appeared. A woman who'd been in front of Sarah in line gave my sister the ticket she'd already bought for her own daughter and then purchased her child a new one.

So Sarah made it to South Station, where she discovered there were no more buses heading west for the night and realized that she now simply wanted to be safe. She no longer cared if she was caught. It was dark outside and the station was closing up. She must have looked terrified and lost, because that's when her "angel two" approached, in the form of a stranger who luckily happened to be a Good Samaritan and not an ax murderer. He took Sarah to McDonald's and bought her an order of french fries and helped her call 411 to track down our third sister, the natural nurturer. The natural nurturer lives only twenty minutes outside Boston, and in less than half an hour she arrived, heavily pregnant and in tears, at South Station, where she scooped Sarah into her arms and brought her home for a cup of tea and warm shelter.

Sarah tells me this whole story while she's still at our sister's house the next day. She's gathering her strength to take one final bus, back home to the Berkshires, anxious to complete the loop she started more than twenty-four hours earlier. She says that after today she's done traveling for a while.

"I know, I know," she says to me before I can make any comments. "You're just glad to hear that I'm alive, you forgive me but I shouldn't do it again, you really love me, you're only trying to help, blah, blah, blah. I've already heard it from Mom and Dad."

I really do love her, I really am trying to help, yet I get the sense that I'm the only one in the family who's pretty thrilled about all of this. My mother, sister, and father are gravely shaken, and even Sarah still appears to be in shock. It hadn't occurred to her that her plan might go awry. She never thought this guy would stand her up–again. Most important, it never crossed her mind that she'd be caught and that all of us, two sisters plus her parents, plus all of her friends and supervisors in the Berkshires, would know that she'd gone AWOL for the day. Yet other than her ego, no one had been hurt. Okay, she didn't get to sing in a parade or drive a 1961 Ferrari 250 GT California, but she did boldly prove that she can veer off course and live to tell about it.

A short while later, when she's able to reflect on the adventure, I ask her if she's seen *Ferris Bueller*.

"Whoa," she says. "That's an oldie."

To Sarah, Matthew Broderick is the voice behind Simba in the film version of *The Lion King*. She was only five when *Ferris Bueller* hit theaters. She grew up in the post-Hughes era, first on animated musicals and then on a new wave of teen flicks that set high schoolers back a few decades. In Sarah's generation's teen movies the geeks and nerds sometimes still win out in the end, but only after they get hipper haircuts and new personalities and quit the marching band. Hughes's lesson that everyone is okay had been supplanted by the idea that with cosmetic help anyone can be all right.

"I didn't really like that movie, *Ferris Bueller*," she tells me, though she remembers it clearly and seems ready to laugh at her own escapade finally. She seems ready to take risks herself again, albeit with more backup cash in her pocket and a phone call home first, to alert the family to her plans. I want to talk to her about Ferris's bravado and the way that she, like Cameron, has broken out of her box–and she only wants to discuss the way the Buellers' dog gnaws at Ed Rooney's leg.

Her boredom with the movie stems from the fact that, as she sees it, everyone these days cuts school. Her generation doesn't need a movie as its touchstone when it comes to being crafty and not getting caught. They don't need a character to represent freedom and scheming. Getting away with things isn't a sport anymore, it's become a fact of life–for kids, and for the adults who influence them. That may be wrong and dangerous, but for now I'm simply thrilled that my own sister, a girl who some onlookers might accuse of being behind the eight ball, isn't afraid to join in.

Real Men Don't Eat Quiche

THE WOES OF FERRIS BUELLER AND
HIS NORTH SIDE BUDDIES

by John McNally

The summer *Ferris Bueller's Day Off* was released, I was twenty years old, living in Carbondale, Illinois, and I was hanging out with a group of friends, some of whom were selling drugs out of our complex. The building had been under police surveillance for months, a squad car frequently stationed across from my friend's blue Chevy Malibu. *I* wasn't selling any drugs, but I often sampled the goods. It was the summer between my junior and senior years of college at Southern Illinois University, and I wanted to be a writer. Between marathon–sometimes drug-induced–typing sessions I would drift outside and play Hacky Sack with my stoner buddies. Talking Heads' *Stop Making Sense* blasted from the speaker parked in front of my open apartment door. We each held a forty-ounce bottle of Mickey's malt liquor, an obstacle that we saw not so much as pathetic as challenging. One of us would kick the Hacky Sack over another person's head and then watch that person chase it, giant bottle of beer in hand, with the futile goal of kicking it back over his own head without tripping or dropping his drink. I think we thought we were funny, but I'm sure we were the only ones who thought so.

My other clear memory of that summer is being dead broke, mostly because of the daily gallons of beer that I was consuming, but also because of the occasional drugs I would buy when my friends' stock ran low. It didn't help that I was prone to do ridiculously impulsive things when I was tripping on shrooms, like calling people I didn't know in France to try out my French. (The French, to their credit, were always polite.) To make ends meet that summer, I lived frugally on a steady diet of potpies and grilled cheese sandwiches. I went to bars and ate the popcorn. I hitchhiked everywhere. But I also ran a number of low-grade scams. I kited checks around town. I found empty beer pitchers at bars and returned them for the dollar deposit when the pitcher's rightful owner wasn't looking. At one of my regular bars I stared longingly into the hot dog carousel and asked what would happen to all those sweating dogs at the end of the night, then offered to buy one at half price, emptying my pockets of whatever spare change and lint remained. By the end of the summer the bartender began offering me a hot dog for the road, but only after announcing last call. He had his principles.

It wasn't the last time in my life that I would hit rock bottom, but it was definitely the lowest I had sunk up until that point.

Ferris Bueller's Day Off opened on June 11, 1986. I caught a weekday matinee at the Saluki, the theater that abutted our apartment complex. There were only ten or so other moviegoers in attendance. I had probably kited a check to pay for admission and an extra-large Coke to get me through my daily hangover.

As soon as Ferris Bueller turned to the camera and began addressing me, that was it: The movie had won me over. Completely! Ferris was the high school student that I had longed to be. Never mind that Matthew Broderick, who plays Ferris, was a twenty-four-year-old man playing an eighteen-year-old boy. Never mind that I was three years out of high school myself. I was still close enough to the raw nerve of adolescence to wish that I could give it another go and maybe get it right this time.

So, what was it precisely that drew me into the movie?

My life in high school—college, too, for that matter—was the antithesis of Ferris's life. I grew up on Chicago's working-class Southwest Side, having spent most of my life in one grubby apartment building after another; Ferris comes from the clean, manicured lawns of upper-class suburban Chicago, namely Northbrook, where most of John Hughes's characters spring from. I drove a four-door Chevelle that had been given to me after my parents' friends' grandfather died; Ferris's friend Cameron lives in a house with an entire showroom of rare and restored cars, including the 1961 Ferrari 250 GT that Ferris talks Cameron into using. Ferris has a state-of-the-art stereo; in 1986, I was still using the receiver and tape deck that came with my 1979 Soundesign stereo unit. Ferris's friends have names like Cameron and Sloane; my high school buddies were Joe and Laura. My father was a roofer and my mother, who used to work in a factory, was on disability; Ferris's father works in a white-collar office in a high-rise downtown, while his mother sells real estate. The list goes on.

On the surface the draw of most John Hughes movies would appear to be the theme of teenage angst, but the *real* pull of his movies—*Ferris Bueller's Day Off* in particular—is wish fulfillment. We *want* to be those kids. Even when they're not having a good time, even when they're going through the worst bouts of teen torment imaginable, their lives are still cooler than ours will ever be. It's not just that the kids are prettier than most of us ever were, or funnier, or more clever; it's that everything will be okay for them, which means that maybe—*maybe*—everything will be okay for us, too. We can project into their futures and see that they, these John

Hughes kids, even the worst of the lot, are going to be all right. Most are destined for big things. Their worries are short-term.

Take Ferris Bueller's best friend, Cameron Frye. What's his problem? Well, his father loves material things more than his own son. Cameron himself, as a result, is a ball of mixed emotions: rage one moment, catatonic silence the next. When Cameron's father's car—the car he and his friends have spent the day joyriding in—flies out of the showroom window and falls several stories to its demise, we may think, *Oh, shit,* but we know deep down that Cameron's going to be okay. The car may be demolished, but you *know* Cameron's father had that baby insured to the hilt. So what's the worst that's going to happen to him? I mean, *really.* Will he be cut out of his father's will? Of course not. Will he end up kicked out of his home for standing up to his father? Heavens, no. He'll probably go on to Harvard in the fall or, in a worst-case scenario, nearby Northwestern. Poor kid.

For Hughes the key to making a successful wish-fulfillment movie like *Ferris Bueller's Day Off* lies in socioeconomics. All of the kids in *Ferris Bueller—all of them*—have financial safety nets. At the end of the day they'll still return to their parents' multimillion-dollar homes. They'll be okay.

I'm sure, on that day way back in 1986 in the Saluki movie theater, I was initially hooked by all the quirkiness of the movie: Ferris Bueller addressing me from the screen while bullet-pointed words appear alongside him; his mugging for the camera, as if he were in a Molière farce; the then-cool sound track, most notably the song "Oh Yeah" by Yello; the blurring of fantasy and reality (Ferris's spur-of-the-moment appearance on a parade float in downtown Chicago while lip-synching a perfectly choreographed "Twist and Shout" that engages everyone watching and inspires pedestrians to dance); the movie continuing even as the credits roll, allowing us to watch nemesis Principal Rooney's ongoing humiliations, which include sitting next to the dorkiest girl on the bus. I'm sure it *all* appealed to me. But it appealed to me because I aspired not only to the charms of Ferris, but to his family's wealth. I wanted the security that Ferris had—the parents who didn't argue, the house loaded with electronic accoutrements, the cool clothes. I knew (or thought I knew) that with money came security, and so I wanted to *be* Ferris. It was that simple.

If you didn't grow up in Chicago, you may not understand that the divide between the North Side and the South Side goes beyond Cubs-Sox rivalry. It's a class war. South Siders tend to see themselves as salt-of-the-earth, meat-and-potatoes working-class folks. To many South Siders, North Siders are elitists who live in a bubble and don't understand how the real world works—in short, educated fools. North Siders, on the other hand, see themselves as both progressive and upwardly mobile, the sort of people who can enjoy a baseball game as well as an opera. To many North Siders, the South Side is another planet, the land of loud, Schlitz-swilling rednecks who would rather fight than talk. These are generalities, of course, but having grown up on the South Side and then lived as an adult on the North Side, I know there's a whiff of truth in all of these presumptions. It didn't seem the least bit odd to me that my high school's homecoming slogan the year we played Evanston (the epitome of North Side snobbery—or so I had been told) was "Real men don't eat quiche!" Nor was it odd that the football coach encouraged this animosity toward the North Side. It all seemed as natural to me as breathing.

As much as I had learned to hate the North Side, I was always jealous when our Speech Team went to one of their high schools for a tournament. Compared with our grubby prison of a building, a North Side high school seemed an oasis, the beacon of progress.

The kids looked smarter, were better dressed, and had better manners. Even the lighting in the hallways was brighter. More sun flowed into the rooms. And there was always something more interesting to look at out their windows than brown grass or power lines.

Recently I was looking over the address book for my graduating high school class's twentieth reunion, and not a single classmate out of more than four hundred had a North Side address. A few had moved to Chicago proper, but no one was living in Evanston, Winnetka, or Northbrook. These are the sorts of neighborhoods where you need to be grandfathered in. The fact that most of my classmates remained not only in Chicago but in the basic area where we grew up speaks volumes about the ways in which socio-economics really work in this country. It's hard to improve your lot in life. Often when your parents' lot is on the lower rung, you're more likely to remain on that rung—or move down a notch or two.

To ignore the class dynamic in Hughes's work is to miss the bigger picture, since North Side Chicago (Northbrook, to be precise) is Hughes's turf. To a South Sider, his movies are fantasies. But of all of John Hughes's movies, *Ferris Bueller's Day Off* really ratchets up the fantasy quotient by making Ferris himself invincible. Ferris can do no wrong. He controls every aspect of his own little universe. His inventions, such as the weight-and-pulley dummy in his bed, are pure genius. Ferris is one half Machiavelli, one half MacGyver. Not only does Ferris have a gorgeous girlfriend, but he never has to worry that she's going to leave him. In fact, nothing is a genuine threat to Ferris. The principal, who is literally hunting Ferris, never really comes close. Perhaps the closest call for Ferris is when he is parked next to his own father in downtown Chicago. The father looks over and *thinks* he sees Ferris, but Ferris has disappeared by the time he does a double take. Or maybe it's at the end of the movie, when his sister spies him walking while she's driving with their oblivious mother in the passenger seat. Jeanie (Jennifer Grey) tries to beat him home. Ferris has no choice but to run through strangers' houses and cut through their backyards. But even while being chased, he has time to charm two sunbathing girls. Will Ferris get caught? Of course not! He's perfect. What teenager–hell, what drug-addled twenty-year-old sitting in the Saluki movie theater in Carbondale, Illinois–*wouldn't* have wanted to be Ferris Bueller, that luckiest of bastards?

But we all grow up. Most of us do, at least.

I watched *Ferris Bueller* several more times on VHS in the three or four years after its release. Eventually, though, it fell out of rotation altogether, as did many movies from that period. In the ensuing years I got married, divorced, married again. My mother died. My father took an early retirement, filed for bankruptcy, and moved into a camping trailer in southern Illinois. I earned an MFA in creative writing and later, because I couldn't find gainful employment, a PhD. I worked a lot of crappy jobs, sometimes as many as three at once, all without benefits. I wrote three unpublished novels. I sold plasma during the lean years. The interest on my student loan debt continued to capitalize while in deferment, to the point that I may now never live long enough to pay it off. In short, life chugged along–and when something truly good happened, it was usually after long periods in which not much had happened at all.

Unlike Ferris, I never had a safety net. If I was broke, I was broke. There was no one to turn to, really. My father helped out when he could, but he himself was bringing in less than four hundred dollars a month during those first few years of his retirement. One time, while driving the six hours from Carbondale to Chicago, I stopped off in Benton, which was where my father's trailer was. I didn't have enough money for gas and thought I could bum ten bucks. The truth is, I didn't have *any* money. Not a dime. My father wasn't home, so I rooted through some old boxes of mine until, at long last, I found a savings bond that had been a gift for my eighth-grade confirmation. The bond hadn't yet matured. Mice had nibbled away its corners. I took it to the bank and collected nearly thirty bucks. In that moment—accepting the cash from the teller—I felt richer than I had ever felt before or, for that matter, since. Not only could I fill up my car with gas, I could eat. And I could eat well, too. I remember topping off my meal with a large milk shake.

Things are better now. I've caught a few lucky breaks here and there. I landed a decent job. The debts still hover, but when don't they?

I watched *Ferris Bueller* again this year for the first time in more than a decade. I was looking forward to it, hoping it hadn't become dated. I was hoping, I suppose, to experience anew what I had experienced in that theater all those years ago. The movie's dialogue came back to me a split second before it was spoken. I even anticipated moments I didn't especially care for the first time around, as when Cameron, while talking to Principal Rooney on the phone, does an impression of Sloane's father that sounds (weirdly) like John Lennon.

What I didn't expect, however, was the resentment I felt toward these characters. I had no sympathy for most of them, including Cameron. John Hughes cheats us, I realize now, because we never *see* Cameron's cruel father, who is characterized as a one-dimensional bad guy. We're supposed to dislike him because we're *told* to dislike him. As a result Cameron now came across as self-indulgent. Had I been Ferris, I would have left Cameron's sorry ass at the bottom of the pool after he had fallen forward in his melodramatic catatonia and sunk to the bottom. It's possible that my lack of sympathy has to do with the rise of victim TV (think Maury Povich, think Sally Jessy

Raphaël) as well as the victim memoir, culminating in the James Frey fiasco. So maybe my patience is a little thin when a rich kid claims that his daddy doesn't love him enough. "Buck up," I wanted to tell Cameron this time around. "No one's father loves him enough. Live with it."

And what's up with the white characters asking the minority characters if they understand English? Was this an easy laugh in the eighties? It happens once when Ferris asks the parking-lot attendant if he understands English. You could argue, I suppose, that the parking-lot attendant has the last laugh by taking the car out for a spin. But when in a later scene Ferris's sister asks someone on the phone if he understands English, I couldn't help but cringe. The little bit of compassion I might have felt for these spoiled kids evaporated entirely. (The Asian character of Long Duk Dong in Hughes's *Sixteen Candles* is even more disturbing. Were the eighties really all that long ago?)

Ironically, the only character for whom I had genuine sympathy this time around was Principal Rooney, the movie's supposed villain. He is the only character who wants to make people accountable for their actions, and he's the only one who genuinely seems to suffer during the course of the film. Unlike with Cameron's woes, which we must take on faith, we actually get to *see* the lack of respect Rooney gets. We *see* the airheaded secretary he must deal with day in, day out. Most of all, we *see* his fruitless plight, from beginning to end. For me, Rooney redeems the movie—perhaps not entirely, but I at least walked away feeling sorry for *one* character. And the movie's ending is truly more honest, more earned, than any other moment that precedes it. I felt nothing but compassion for this guy who, after getting his shitty car towed away, is humiliated by having to take the school bus home, and who, while sitting next to the school dork, finds profane graffiti that insults him by name. What was this man's crime?

Attempting to instill responsibility in a bunch of spoiled brats? Is that so bad?

If John Hughes wants to make a truly honest movie, I have a pitch for him. Let's call this one *Principal Rooney's Day Off*, and let's pick it up in 2006. Ferris and his buddies are well into their careers as CEOs, film producers, or trust-fund slackers. Life has been good; life has been sweet. Cut to Principal Rooney: He's in his midsixties now and beaten down by an unfulfilled life. A life of dealing with Bueller clones has left him at loose ends. A life of working with his nutty secretary has made him a little nutty himself. Maybe one night in a bar, after downing one too many shots, Rooney strikes up a conversation with another fellow, a man who has spent the past twenty years working as a parking-garage attendant. When the attendant tells the story of the day he went joyriding in a 1961 Ferrari 250 GT, Rooney's eyes light up. He *knows* that car. How strange, they realize, that their seemingly different lives once intersected! They drink some more; they pull their barstools closer. Eventually they hatch a plan. And this time, well, this time Ferris had better watch his ass. This time he might not be so lucky.

Now, *that's* a movie I'd pay ten bucks to see.

I Dated Molly Ringwald, Sort Of

by Dan Pope

The first glimpse comes in *Sixteen Candles,* just after the opening titles. You see her from behind, looking at herself in the mirror. She is wearing a slip. Then comes the close-up of her face. Those big brown eyes. The red hair. But most of all, the pouty mouth—round and small, the inexplicably full lips, a slight overbite. She strikes a Hollywood pose, then drops it.

"Hopeless," she tells herself.

I was a college student then, in 1984. The movie was entertaining in a benign sort of way, but I was a tad too old for teenage angst. (I was taking a European-film course; I recall telling friends, "I only watch movies with subtitles.")

But whenever Molly Ringwald came on screen, I was hooked.

She was best, of course, with John Hughes. Like Scorsese and De Niro, they clicked. In the trilogy—*Sixteen Candles* (1984), *The Breakfast Club* (1985), *Pretty in Pink* (1986)—she plays a variation of the same role: the suburban everygirl (she's middle class in the first film, upper class in the second, and "poor" in the third). She's in nearly every frame of all three films, and when she's not, you feel her absence.

She is innocent yet knowing, sincere yet sarcastic. She isn't sexy, but there is something sexy about her. She's buddingly sexual, more interested in love than lust. She is all about the high school crush, the dream guy.

She follows the rules. When her parents forget her sixteenth birthday, she doesn't get mad. She rolls her eyes heavenward and laments, "I can't believe they fucking forgot my birthday." It's that "fucking" that is so incongruous, that gets the laugh. Because Molly is always the good girl.

A virgin.

She doesn't complain about her parents, like her cohorts in the Hughes movies. She has heart-to-hearts with her father, both in *Sixteen Candles* and *Pretty in Pink*, discussing boy problems.

Harry Dean Stanton plays her unemployed dad in *Pretty in Pink*. He's supposed to be likable but poor, a slacker single parent, but perhaps John Hughes miscast this role. Stanton, with his greasy grin and two-day stubble, looks like he just wandered off the set of a David Lynch movie. There's something creepy about his boyish haircut and the way he keeps hugging his daughter. Yet Molly bounds joyfully into his bedroom to wake him in the morning, throws open the curtains, offers to make him breakfast. "Come on," she says. "Get up."

She's not exactly pretty. Her smile is gummy. Her chin juts out too far, ruining her profile. You don't want to like her. You want to dislike her because you are *supposed* to like her, like the latest boy band.

Yet she is irresistible.

The way she squints when annoyed.

The way she rolls her eyes heavenward in exasperation.

The way she bites her bottom lip when deep in thought.

And, may I say again, that mouth. Watch her—just for a split second—in *The Breakfast Club*, whistling. I replay that moment again and again, like the Zapruder film, trying to fathom its ineffability.

She's most affecting when lovelorn. "Don't fall in love," she tells her dog in *Pretty in Pink*, resting her forehead against the dog's head. "You just won't like it. It's *very* complicated."

Most will recall her signature moments.

Say, in *Sixteen Candles*, when her grandmother reaches out and squeezes her breasts. "I can't believe my grandmother actually felt me up," she says.

Or in *The Breakfast Club*, when she puts on her lipstick without using her hands; or later, in the same film, when she dances her eighties dance at the top of the library stairs, alone. (I love those suede boots.)

Yet I'm drawn to her more-quiet moments.

In *Sixteen Candles* there's the scene in the classroom where she turns in her seat to a sneak a glance at Jake Ryan, the boy she adores from afar. It seems to happen in slow motion. Turning to her left, she raises her eyes toward him, blinks, registers that he is gorgeous, notices after a moment that he is looking back, pretends that she is not looking at him—she is just scratching her chin against her shoulder—then shyly turns back toward the front of the classroom, simultaneously blissful at the sight of him and horrified that he has caught her staring. He is a senior; she is a lowly sophomore.

Later we see her standing fully clothed outside the shower in the girls' locker room, admiring the blond prom queen—Jake Ryan's girlfriend—who is soaping herself under the water (a rare moment of nudity in early Hughes). Cut to Molly. Look at the intensity of her gaze, that brown-eyed concentration. "It's unbelievable," she says, sizing up her competition. "She's perfect."

And later that night she stands on the sidelines in the school gymnasium, watching Jake Ryan slow-dance with his prom queen. As Molly studies them, she lets her mouth fall slightly open. Just a quarter inch, her lips part. But it is incredibly stirring, that slight parting, which seems to acknowledge the extent of her reverie for his athletic good looks and the impossibility of her crush on him.

"He doesn't even know I exist," she complains.

The Hughes trilogy of the mid-eighties is a veritable treasure trove of bad fashion. The big hair. The cutoff T-shirts and baggy pants. The layering of garments. The clothes signify one's clique. In *Pretty in Pink* the poor kids wear mismatched outfits and hats, while the "richies" wear sport coats.

Yet Molly seems less a fashion victim than her costars. That neat bob is timeless. It still looks good. Her hair is a dark red in *Sixteen Candles*, a shade lighter in *The Breakfast Club*, and lighter still, and slightly teased, in *Pretty in Pink*.

Granted, the pink prom dress she wears in *Pretty in Pink* is not pretty at all. It's an unmitigated disaster. But other than that, her attire is cute in a thrown-together, thrift-shop, Annie Hall sort of way, all floppy skirts, button-front blouses, vests, and, yes, hats.

Compare her girlfriend at the record store in *Pretty in Pink*—we first meet her in a full-blown mohawk—or anything worn by dear Duckie in that same film to get an idea how bad one could look in the mid-eighties, seemingly without knowing it. (Were we blind then? Did we really dress like that? Did we tease our hair into those fantastic configurations?)

"You really don't think she's got something?" Andrew McCarthy asks in *Pretty in Pink*.

Yes, it is undeniable, that something. It's in the twinkle of her eye, the pout of her lips. Ringlets, as her legion of adolescent female fans were called, aped her every move. She made the cover of *Time* magazine in 1986.

The future couldn't have looked any brighter.

• • •

Cut to 1993. I'm living in Hartford, Connecticut, house-sitting an empty, beaten-down Tudor mansion. The house has sixteen rooms and nine bathrooms, and I am the sole occupant. (The owners pay all the expenses, including a stipend for my board.)

I'm not working very much, although I tell people I'm a freelance writer. I have vague ambitions to be a novelist, but mostly I play basketball, get drunk, sleep late. The house-sitting gig was supposed to last six months, but it stretches to three and a half years, and with the extended tenancy my life has become a sort of never-never land of big-screen television and empty rooms.

Then I meet Molly Ringwald's double.

This happens at a house party in the West End. She is standing in the center of the crowded living room, wearing tight jeans and a tighter sweater, slugging Budweiser out of a bottle. I do a double take. She has the same pouty lips, the same googly brown eyes, the same full cheeks—everything but the red hair. (Hers is black and curly.) She even has the same bright smile, performs the patented Ringwald eye rolls.

I go over to introduce myself. When I mention her resemblance to Molly R., she says, "Yeah, I get that a lot. But I like it better when people say Andie MacDowell."

I don't ask for her phone number. But we have a mutual friend, so I know how to get in touch with her.

Over the next three weeks I do some investigating. I don't want to blow my chance. I find out where she lives, where she works, where she works out. She has no boyfriend, I quickly learn.

Looking back now, I recall moments of something close to insanity. Lying in bed for hours on end, unable to sleep, plotting how to see her next. It seemed too simple to pick up the phone and call her. No. She might not remember me. It might be awkward. Rather, I try to arrange "chance meetings"—by going to the Ralph

Lauren store in the mall, where she works for extra cash a few nights a week. After a half hour lurking outside the entranceway, I summon my courage. I have on my best jeans. My hair is slicked and pomaded like Duckie's.

I enter the store, pluck a polo shirt off the display rack, carry it to the cash register, and–

"Hey," she says.

"Oh," I say, trying to act nonchalant. "You work here?"

"Monday and Wednesday nights."

"Wow, I didn't know."

Then comes the John Hughes moment–the shy smiles, the blushing, the looking down at one's feet. We don't know what to say next.

I blurt out, "Do you like the color of this shirt?"

"Yes. Purple would look good on you."

"Thanks."

"You're Dan. We met at that party."

The fact that she remembers my name gives me hope. As she folds my shirt and charges my credit card, I take my shot:

"Do you want to grab a drink after your shift?"

At T.G.I. Friday's we gorge on chicken wings and Rolling Rock. In the parking lot I shake her hand good night, and she gives me her phone number. It is a success, I think.

But later that night, getting ready for bed, I get hit with a fever. It comes on suddenly. I shiver and shake. My chest feels hot to the touch. I am more thirsty than I can recall ever being, but when I crawl to the bathroom, the water tastes like metal and I spit it out. I crunch up some aspirin and take my temperature. It's 104. Delirium follows. Sometime near dawn the fever breaks, like a weight being removed from my chest.

The next day a doctor tells me I have pneumonia.

I spend a week in bed and another few days stumbling around the house, feeling pale and miserable.

Then comes the next John Hughes moment. I'm talking on the phone to the mutual friend, and she says, "Oh, there's something else. I probably shouldn't tell you this."

"Tell me what?"

"She's wondering when you're going to call. She has a *wicked crush* on you."

Cue the Psychedelic Furs or Orchestral Manoeuvers in the Dark—or any of those dreamy bands that Hughes used to score his films—and watch me, like dear Duckie, dancing soundlessly around the room, pumping my fist and doing karate kicks.

"Really?" I say.

"Yeah. You must have known."

"Well, no. Not really."

The usual stuff follows. We go to movies, get drunk, kiss, fuck, take showers together, move in. She meets my parents. I meet hers. We vacation on the Cape. I tell her I love her. She tells me in a baby voice, "Di dove do"—which I take to mean the same thing.

But then the summer ends and so does anything resembling a John Hughes movie.

We are over, another relationship through. She moves to New York City, and I stay behind in my empty mansion.

I once thought I would be married by thirty. That kids would follow. That I would be a productive member of literary society. Her absence makes it clear to me that none of this has happened or will happen soon. Depression ensues.

Later I wonder, *Why did it hurt so excessively when she left? Why did I write letters to her for years afterward without getting a single response? Why am I writing this about her now?*

• • •

In a John Hughes movie you never learn how things turn out. There's no epilogue, no moment of recognition, as in *American Graffiti*, that these teens will meet the future, that life awaits them.

So here is how it turned out, courtesy of Google.

I start with my ex, my Molly doppelgänger. She produces only a single hit: her name in a list of college alumni. Nothing further, just her name. A single hit is not impressive. What has she done with her life to so completely avoid the reach of Google?

Next I go to a find-a-person Web site. When I type in her name, a list of addresses pops up. Here are all the residences of her life. I have been to a few of them: her parents' house in upstate New York; her college apartment in Springfield, Massachusetts; the house she rented in Hartford, where we met during the summer of 1993; and five or six different addresses in New York City—where she apparently still lives.

Her age is listed on the Web site as thirty-seven. That seems strange and disconcerting. I knew her when she was twenty-five. She's twenty-five in all the pictures I have of her, twenty-five in my mind. This is a common trick of memory. Molly Ringwald, also age thirty-seven as I write this—she was born on February 18, 1968, in Roseville, California—is sixteen in our collective memory, sweet sixteen and pretty in pink forever.

For a one-time payment of $19.95, I can get complete access to all public documents relating to my ex, including real estate records, criminal court records, documents relating to birth and death, marriage and divorce, motor vehicle records, tax liens and judgments, possible relatives, aliases, neighbors, DEA registrants, and Web site ownership, if any such records exist.

I am tempted to plunk down the dough and learn more.

But no.

Better that she remain unmarried, undivorced, untethered by liens and judgments, unknown to the present. Better that she remain twenty-five.

When I knew her, her aspiration was to become a famous criminal defense lawyer. She wanted to travel the country representing the underprivileged and wrongly accused, like Clarence Darrow and William Kunstler.

But maybe that didn't happen. Maybe her life has been unaccomplished. Maybe she met a nice fellow, married, reproduced. Maybe she spends her time chasing her children around a New York brownstone. Maybe she put on weight.

And what became of Molly, the *real* Molly, not my pale imitation?

According to Leonard Maltin, "bad choices and bad luck" fizzled her career. She once had Hollywood in the palm of her hand. But look what happened: She turned down the Julia Roberts role in *Pretty Woman*. Turned down the Demi Moore role in *Ghost*. Refused the Lea Thompson role in *Some Kind of Wonderful*, ending her collaboration with John Hughes. David Lynch wanted her to play the Laura Dern role in *Blue Velvet*; he sent her the script, but Molly's mother read it first, found it disturbing, and never showed the script to her daughter.

The movies she made after 1990—can you name one?—are godawful: B-rate slasher films and police dramas. See if you can sit through one to the end. In *Cut* (2000) she looks, well, a bit overweight. And definitely not sixteen.

But her biography reveals a nice-sounding life, if not an impressive film career. She moved to France in 1992, likes to cook and read, writes short stories, lives with a writer/editor, acts on the London stage, had a baby girl in 2003.

Life turns out differently than we once expected.

This happens to all of us.

Never count a man happy until the day of his death, said the Greeks.

So what if Molly turned down some pretty choice roles?

So what if she peaked early?

Hemingway did his best work before he was thirty. Ditto Fitzgerald. Ditto Einstein, for that matter. What more need one do in a life after figuring out that $E = mc^2$? Or writing *The Sun Also Rises* or *The Great Gatsby*? Or starring in three of the greatest teen movies ever made?

We don't reach the heights we once thought we would. We fall out of love, get divorced, suffer liens and judgments, eat too much, get soft around the middle. But so what? We were once young, and maybe beautiful, and maybe in love.

The Ghost of Ally Sheedy

by Lewis Robinson

When I was fourteen, my friends and I were addicted to poker. At school we played during every free period. We played after classes, too, and on the weekends. We called one another by last name (Rollins, Dunn, Zielinski, and Robinson), and we played for actual currency (nickels, dimes, and quarters–each of us kept a stash of loose change). When my parents left town, we gathered at the kitchen table and for hours on end we played cards. If someone brought cigars, we'd smoke them.

Zielinski rubbed his chin when he held aces, and he stacked his coins in neat little piles. Dunn was prone to making large bets on small odds; unpredictability was his signature. We knew it gave Rollins much more pleasure to win with a pair of threes than with a straight flush; he relished a good bluff. Money changed hands between us often without any of us suffering significant losses. In the long run the four of us more or less broke even. The only times we noticed any real influx of cash was when we invited someone outside our regular foursome to play. That's when we'd all see a little bump in our earnings. I suppose we should have been looking to invite more outsiders to our table, but for some reason we had very specific ideas about how the game should be conducted. We didn't want to explain our rules. Playing with people who talked too much or sang the Kenny Rogers song was out of the question. Also--and I'm not sure where we picked up this charming piece of wisdom--

girls were not fit to play poker. Unfortunately, our no-girls policy applied to many aspects of our life. Smoking pot was a boys-only activity. Tackle football on the lawn in front of the school was another favorite pastime—no girls allowed. We even went to the mall without girls. Rollins had once had sex with a girl, and Dunn and Zielinski and I were interested in such a possibility, but actually doing it was far beyond our powers of imagination.

That fall I went to see *The Breakfast Club*. For a fourteen-year-old kid who was devoted to a certain code of teenage behavior, the movie felt like a sacred text. In the back of my mind I knew I looked like Anthony Michael Hall, but I fancied myself as the Judd Nelson character, John Bender. All of us did. Bender is a badass. He rips up books in the library. He keeps his boots untied. He makes the main adult in the movie (Richard Vernon, played by the late Paul Gleason) look like a spineless idiot. The story is set in Illinois, just outside Chicago, but my friends and I knew that Judd Nelson had grown up in Maine—he'd attended our rival school—and this made him all the more real. The only thing I didn't see eye to eye with Bender about was that at the end of the movie he chooses Claire (Molly Ringwald) over Allison (Ally Sheedy). This seemed unconscionable. Claire is the whiny popular girl whose greatest talent is being able to apply lipstick without using her hands. Allison, conversely, opened my eyes to a whole new category of female. She steals, lies, and throws lunch meat in the air. She makes a sandwich out of Pixy Stix and Cap'n Crunch. She keeps her purse full of necessities so that she's prepared to flee the scene (her house, her school, the country) at any moment. Here, finally, was a girl who would have been welcome at our poker table. Her beauty and her recalcitrance made me understand why pursuing the opposite sex would be a top priority for the next few decades. After seeing the movie, I devoted my life to finding a girl like her.

• • •

It didn't take me long to realize that high school was the wrong time for such a quest. I carried my virginity to college like a flag at half-mast. When I first arrived at Middlebury College, I knew right away that things would be different. Someone in the Dean's Office had made a mistake and put me in a hall with all seniors. My roommate (a God-fearing baseball star from Texas) and I lived near a drunk guy who wore a kilt, broke empty bottles against the wall, and cried himself to sleep. Another senior two doors down, Stan, had a long beard and played his guitar in the stairwell. He became my mentor, explaining to me the tacit rules of college life. He worked at the campus radio station, so I started working there too. He was friends with people in the Theater Department, and he introduced them to me. His girlfriend was a poet. Stan told me, "There are two kinds of women. The safe, girl-next-door types, like your mom." He scratched his beard and gazed off into space. "And then there are the wild ones."

Around this time I had also reconnected with an acquaintance from Maine who lived in a freshman dorm. She was Ringwaldian in her tastes and her attitude, but her roommate was a dark-eyed poet with a devilish grin. The roommate's name was Lila. She was quick witted and sarcastic and slightly mean. She had a boyfriend, of course, a guy named Quentin who didn't go to college; he was a muscled artist-type who was squatting in an abandoned building in Brooklyn. I became friends with Lila right away, and my obsession with Ally Sheedy was quickly and efficiently transferred. Lila had a big snarl of brown hair and beautiful skin. She wrote a lot of poetry, and when she found out that I wrote fiction, she said, "That's good practice for when you're ready to graduate to the poetic form." Her confidence excited me. I met Quentin a few times—he was a surly lug—but his visits always ended and then he was gone, back on the

Greyhound to New York, at which point I could continue to suggest, subtly, that Lila should leave him and be with me. Miraculously, it didn't take long for these suggestions to get some traction. She told me that Quentin was sexy but he was dark and brooding and didn't treat her especially well. She told me that he was a champion in the sack but he wasn't always nice. I didn't like hearing about his sexual prowess, but I was happy to capitalize on his shortcomings, and when, on a stormy afternoon, she finally told me it was over between them, I pounced. Actually, it was she who did the pouncing; I had already pounced (emotionally) long ago, and she knew it. As for making a move, I was too inexperienced, so I had to follow her lead. She was happy to play this role. She'd moved into an all-girls dorm and no longer had a roommate. She introduced me, finally, to the world of sexual intercourse. For the next few weeks we would make love in the early evening, put our clothes back on, and walk out into the night air. We'd stroll around campus side by side, having just minutes earlier been naked together in the privacy of her room, and I felt drunk and giddy and alive.

Now that I was a kept man, I started noticing things I hadn't noticed when I was merely stalking her. There were several other gentlemen on campus who were obsessed with Lila in the same way I'd been. She enjoyed these attentions; she liked how they kept me on edge. When her suitors left presents outside her door, she laughed. When we were in bed together, she would sometimes tell me about Quentin and his incredible "staying power." I would wrinkle my brow, and she would say, "It's okay, honey, you're just different from him, and that's fine." To keep me from getting too discouraged, she would parcel out compliments for me, too, but then another present from another suitor would arrive.

Apparently Quentin had never really received the message that he and Lila were no longer a couple, and when he found out I was sharing her bed, he borrowed a friend's motorcycle and started driving north. Lila didn't tell me he was on his way until he had just crossed into Vermont and called her from a pay phone. That's when she said he was very angry and it would be better if she talked to him alone.

"I need to face this guy," I said.

"No, you don't. He'll kill you," she said.

"You don't think I need to face him?"

"I need to see him alone," she said.

I honored her request, but I asked her to promise me that she wouldn't sleep with him. She smiled, briefly–how she loved the drama!–and then she promised.

By the end of the year I knew I needed some time away from poetry.

I spent that summer as far from Lila as I could: I drove to Alaska. I got there weeks after the salmon season had started, so the only job I could find was at a cannery in Bethel, in the middle of the tundra. They'd run out of housing, so I pitched a tent outside the cannery and began working twelve-hour shifts, midnight until noon. After work I'd lie in my tent in the hot sun trying to sleep. As soon as I finally dozed off, it was time to wake up and punch the clock. I worked on the line, gutting fish.

Amid the slaughter, spray of hoses, and thunder of hard-driving guitar on the cannery's radio, I noticed that the woman working next to me on the line wore a bandanna, had mischievous eyes, and rarely spoke. I would pass her the fish after cutting them open and scooping out the entrails. She would scrape blood away from their spines. During the course of each twelve-hour shift we would engage in a few clipped conversations. The more I talked to her, the more intrigued I became. One day she talked more openly and told me it had been hard for her to get work since she'd gotten out of prison.

Hook, line, and sinker.

Like the lush who swears off booze after a particularly rough night, my resolve to steer clear of dark-eyed, smirking, roguish women was weak. Here was the pattern: get enthralled, get attached, get overwhelmed, flee, get bored, get enthralled all over again. After many years of this I began to wonder: Did John Hughes have secret voodoo powers? Was he able to identify and supercharge certain clichés so deftly that they were actually affecting my behavior? If he'd structured his plot differently, might I have fallen in love with Molly Ringwald, or Emilio Estevez? Would the sirens of my youth have been redheads, or wearers of varsity letter jackets?

Alas, it was Ally Sheedy who was given *The Breakfast Club*'s best line: "When you grow up, your heart dies." When I heard those words, I anticipated the death of my heart and fiercely wanted to keep it alive. All John Hughes had to do, then, was sprinkle in a little Simple Minds, and I was on my way.

My Mary

by Ben Schrank

In 1987 I was a high school senior in Brooklyn, New York. My friends and I *hated* John Hughes. He had nothing to do with us. We were urban and he was not. We were ironic and he was not. We were going to become artists and he was not an artist. We saw all of his movies anyway. We were moved to tears but would never admit it. We dismissed his efforts but memorized all of his lines.

John Hughes's world was bigger and cleaner and quieter than mine. The people were mostly white, and the landscape was filled with single-family houses and cars and yards with lawns and old green trees. It was a fantasyland for someone else, somebody's apolitical younger sister. But then Hughes showed me Mary Stuart Masterson. She starred in two movies that I loved: James Foley's *At Close Range* and Hughes's *Some Kind of Wonderful.*

Mary had an upturned nose that instantly defined what I felt was unattainable for a Jewish kid from Brooklyn. When she first turned to look at us, in her stupid outfit with the knickers, dragging the drumsticks as if they'd come with her straight from an acting lesson, I knew. From then on I would sing the song of Mary Stuart Masterson. Of course, if I wanted to watch *Some Kind of Wonderful* without constantly having to make fun of it, I had to go to my grandmother's house in Livingston, New Jersey.

At about this time my cousin Ami Cohen died in a car accident. After the funeral, when we were sitting shivah, my

grandfather, who was bigger than James Gandolfini, pulled me into a bathroom and said I was the sole remaining male heir to his name and had better start acting like it. He meant I needed to be more of a Jew. I doubt I said a word, but I did understand that my secret attraction to Mary Stuart Masterson was not what the family wanted. But I didn't care. I wanted to live intensely! With desire, with fear and anxiety and the pressure and madness of young love. I wanted a girl like Mary.

And I found that girl. I met her at the end of my senior year. She was a freshman and as tall as me. She had short hair that she dyed white blond. She wore short skirts and an army jacket that came from Agnès B. in Soho. And her nose turned up dramatically. Her face was pale and her features were far apart. Her lips were pink, and she pushed them forward into a square, pouting frown. She had enormous green eyes. She was rich and lived in Manhattan in a loft. She started at my school in the spring because she'd been kicked out of her last school. I think she was bored and wanted entrée into my gang of guys. I cannot think of another reason why she picked me. But I was happy that she did.

We took her along when we blew off school and went to drink rum and Coke under the Manhattan Bridge. We explored the tunnels that linked the buildings together in Brooklyn Heights. We skateboarded, and she skateboarded too. And through it all she stared at me. She stared at me the way Mary Stuart Masterson stares at Sean Penn in *At Close Range*, the way she stares at Eric Stoltz in *Some Kind of Wonderful*. We would go to parties in the East Village, and she was the one who went through the window and out onto the fire escape, staring back at me to make sure I was following her up, up to the roof, and then she wanted to go higher, always higher, up the ladder to the water tower, up into the teepee-shaped crawl space at the top of the tower and then up and out to climb on the shingles and up to the point above. But I would pull her back. She was fourteen. I didn't want to lose her. I knew I was afraid. I knew she wasn't.

Then my friend Dan Kazin, the craftiest of us all, told us he had figured out how to climb into the enormous uprights that supported the great span of the Manhattan Bridge. He promised to show us, but the time had to be right. One night in May we hung around on the promenade, drinking. We'd begun with twenty people, and by two or so in the morning we were a tighter, drunker group. Finally there were only five of us. Dan said he was ready to take us to the bridge. He asked my Mary if she wanted to come, and she said yes, of course; she was offended by the question and looked to me for support. But I only asked her if she was sure, and then she was annoyed with me, too. We followed Dan.

He showed us how to run along the studded steel roadway until we reached the upright, then throw ourselves down a hole, swing around with nothing but dark water below, and land in an even darker hole, until we got completely inside the upright. Then we had to scamper up the interior ladder, surrounded by rusted, slimy steel, and then, after that endless ascent, come out inside the ten-foot circular iron cage at the top that looked like a ball from the ground, but up there it was really fingers of steel, like an enormous black zucchini blossom that was twenty stories or more above the East River.

Once we'd made it, I cowered inside the steel fingers with my Mary. I swore to both of us that I'd get us home safe, that we wouldn't fall and drown in the East River just because we had wanted to prolong the night, to see how high we could get. She listened, but her eyes were elsewhere. Of course Dan Kazin and the rest of them were swinging on the outside of the fingers by one hand, their whole bodies dangling in the air.

Then everyone but me and my Mary raced down the hundred

yards of thick steel cable that extended from the upright all the way to the bridge span. That cable was about two feet in diameter, and there were two ropes on either side of it. A spot of grease could be the end. But my friends just skidded down as if they were in a Disney movie and the world were safe. They were invisible to the cars below, their bodies far too ready to leave the cable behind and fall down into the East River, their lighters, cigarettes, Vans slip-ons, half-empty cans of Foster's, all of it dropping away from them and foreshadowing the long fall into the cold water that, at that distance, had a surface just as hard as concrete.

I discovered that the safest place to cower was in the middle of the iron beam between the two balls, a space about the size of an army cot. I lay down there and beckoned to my Mary, every digit and limb and even my cheek attached to the freezing metal. Then I demanded that we climb, alone, all the way back down the ladder that was enclosed in the great pillar that supported the cable. I said it was all because I didn't want her to risk her life. But we both knew it was because I was afraid to die.

We came out below the roadway and were dragged up to the relative safety of Manhattan-bound traffic by friends who knew I believed I was doing what was right to protect my Mary and liked me enough not to call me out on how ridiculous I was. These were friends who also knew that she was courageous and that if it hadn't been for me, she would have happily danced down the cable, slid down it on her tiny ass, bouncing and laughing with the guys.

I knew that arguing that I needed to protect my Mary was bullshit. But I had never been so scared in my life. My Mary would do anything. She was so high. But not me. The lifesaver. I hung on to her the way a child hangs on to a doll. At every moment I believed our connection was sublime.

In those movies Mary Stuart Masterson looked at boys and made them think they were better than they really were. She could stare at a boy even when he'd failed and she would engender warmth and confidence. Her eyes were big and warm, and her lips were pushed out and full. She'd look at you and say, "Hey, it's okay that you were a coward just now. I still love you. Someday you'll be big enough to handle the kind of love I have for you. I might even wait for you until then."

But with my Mary it was different. Her therapist, parents, sister, friends, all of them were saying, "Hey, lose the pimpled senior, the dead weight, the jerk who keeps fun to a minimum." They were more than right. I was in love with a haircut, a false promise, a way of being that was illusory, so far from any reality. I sang the song of Mary Stuart Masterson. I indulged in the stupid wish that my Mary could somehow become more innocent. Instead I should have been more courageous.

Mary was like the Mother Teresa of young female actors. John Hughes framed her open gaze and sent it streaming across a screen like a radical act, a nose or a haircut or a way of speaking, a pretty voice on a girl who could not have been less of a tomboy in my eyes. Yes, I guess I thank John Hughes. Because when a girl stares at a boy with eyes that say, *I know you're an idiot, but I love you anyway,* she is looking with Mary's eyes. Months passed and my friends went back to climb the Manhattan Bridge again and again. But not me. Summer came, and my Mary broke up with me.

In *At Close Range*, I remember James Foley's cinematographer lingering over Mary at the fountain in the middle of town, while Sean Penn stares at her and says to himself, "Hey, that's a pretty girl. I could be worthy of a girl like that." Now, I know we were all way too cynical in high school, and we were tougher on one another than we had to be. I miss the way Mary Stuart Masterson looked at boys. But I'm not sorry I didn't run down the cable that suspends the Manhattan Bridge. I don't have great balance, and I do not think I would have made it. I know I lost my Mary that night on the bridge. But the Mary Stuart Masterson who starred in those movies would have understood.

The Scream, with Lip Gloss

by Elizabeth Searle

1. Molly's Mouth and Me

Let's start with lips. Molly's and Macaulay's: different John Hughes films but the same lips, same scream. Molly Ringwald, of course, screamed first.

The first I knew of John Hughes was Molly's mouth. I was too much an outcast in my teens to actually attend cool movies such as Hughes's teen-angst classics. But I knew Molly Ringwald's striking plain/pretty face from my parents' *Time*; I noticed, in those pre-collagen days, the rarity of her pillowy lips.

Before Macaulay Culkin delivered *The Scream* of the '90s on the iconic poster for *Home Alone*, Molly Ringwald in her own Hughes hits screamed for the '80s, for us. When, say, she discovers in *Sixteen Candles* that a seemingly sweet geek has charged admission for boys to view her pink-polka-dotted panties, she makes her full-lipped mouth a black hole of sheerest teen horror.

It is an anguished O; it is a cry of the soulful in the soulless landscape of the early '80s. It is, in short, *The Scream*, with lip gloss.

My own mouth, had I screamed like that at age sixteen, would have been hideously hinged by mini rubber bands attached to my braces. My teeth glittered with metal; my overdone lip gloss gleamed like drool. I practice-kissed my pillow alone in my bedroom, missing out–because I never went out–on the first John Hughes boom. On, especially, his three Molly movies.

With her beyond-bee-stung lips, big eyes, and red-haired bob, Molly Ringwald was our own Clara Bow, our fifteen-minute It Girl. A girl with a woman's mouth. Her face, with its mix of plain and pretty, womanly and girlish, vacuous and canny, emblemized the new teen films pioneered by Hughes: edgy, sexy, painfully realistic yet fanciful. Films I wish I'd seen at the time; films of the time that capture our coming of age, our specifically 1980s brand of angst.

These were the days of MTV, *Miami Vice,* "Material Girl," Metallica–and Molly. Those of us who were young in the neighborhood of the '80s were, as Hughes intuited, a new breed of adultized teen. For middle-class kids like me, restless but well-meaning upwardly mobile parents kept us uprooted, undersupervised, and overfunded. The last of four different high schools I attended made its name in the '80s for a student-run cocaine ring. The walls of our drama room were plastered with overlapping glossy photos cut from *People.* Meryl Streep, Madonna–and Molly.

Without the strictures of the '50s or the idealism of the '60s to rebel against or throw ourselves into, without even the crunchy-granola earnestness of the '70s to ground us, much of our generation drifted in pre-Prozac ennui. As Molly Ringwald in *Sixteen Candles* melodramatically declares: "It is physically impossible for me to get happy." We were, we felt, home alone–together.

2. So Real, So True

What is it about John Hughes and us? What does Hughes capture so well in his slick yet oddly resonant films, in those memorable M. and M. faces? Mirroring each other, and us. Molly's and Macaulay's: both flawed faces by the absurd airbrushed standards of Hollywood today. Both have the expressive, slightly swollen look of babies, with generous noses and mouths. Both mug for the camera with the hammy naturalness of home-movie kids. Maybe Hughes's films, with their all-too-real geeks and acne-pocked adolescents, presaged reality TV.

What's uncanny about young Molly is how she seems—as my husband muttered recently, surprised by the punch *Sixteen Candles* still packs—"so real, so true." The very vacuity of Molly's often-blank stare creates a jolting verisimilitude.

To watch genuine teen Molly Ringwald in *The Breakfast Club* is to watch a real, giggly '80s girl, such as those who scorned me in my various high school halls. To watch the mutable, un-made-up Molly wistfully survey her boyish body in *Sixteen Candles* is, for me, to reconnect with my own gawky yet game high school self. And Molly in *Pretty in Pink*, as the offbeat teen who trumps the mainstream girls at her prom? She, of course, was the me that I—and all "artist" outcasts—wanted to be.

Despite his shameless Cinderella endings, John Hughes in these films peels off the soft-focus gloss that makes many teen films of earlier eras (Elvis, anyone?) feel unreal today. In the process Hughes strikes the sweet-spot jackpot, creating films that could be embraced by both teens and adults at the time, or—as in my case—films to be savored years later by '80s survivors.

How does Hughes hit his (our) pitch-perfect *Scream*?

3. "Only Visiting This Planet"

For starters, John Hughes takes a high school vision a shade less black than Stephen King's in *Carrie* and mixes it with pop effervescence, with cheerfully crude slapstick humor, with unabashed Frank Capra sentimentality. *Carrie* and Capra; puke jokes and pathos. Borrowing gritty realism from breakthrough films of the '70s such as *Carrie* and *American Graffiti*, Hughes captures a teen experience both universal and unique to its times.

And at his best, Hughes the cultural anthropologist makes his precisely observed high school worlds both familiar and strange– especially when seen through the rapt and deeply dazed eyes of Molly Ringwald. Early on in *Sixteen Candles*, Hughes focuses on a trendy button that he might as well have pinned to his heroine as she makes her shaky way through the high school minefields he lays out for her: ONLY VISITING THIS PLANET.

"Turn up the dials," I always advise myself and my writing students when we attempt to capture the moment. But you have to know which dials to twist. And how far to twist them–for Hughes, only too far is enough.

4. "You need four inches of bod"

Teens of any era know their body is no longer their own. It is watched, judged. Especially (take it from me) in the MTV era. Gone was the forgiving, all-natural look of the '70s; the '80s was a time of big hair, hard-edged makeup, Madonna-esque black underwear, worn outside; it was the first era in which ordinary teens, as my grandmother remarked, dressed like "streetwalkers."

Molly Ringwald is equally convincing as a big-haired, glossy-lipped, model-slim beauty in *The Breakfast Club* as she is a tousled-haired waif sizing up her "bod" in her bedroom mirror in *Sixteen Candles*. The latter is the Molly I most relate to: sidelined, shy, waiting out her slow-to-grow body.

Hughes takes the awkwardness all teens feel and amps it up to a new level. His jumpily cut scenes are backed by propulsive punk rock that catches his teens' 1980s-speed minds. Meanwhile, his over-the-top sight gags catch the more timeless klutziness and vulnerability of their bodies.

These are, BTW, real teen bodies: refreshingly unenhanced. Molly sports small, gently curved breasts, not implants. Boys of all shapes and sizes line up hopefully at the dance in *Sixteen Candles*, facing down Hughes's camera, acne and all.

In countless priceless miniscenes John Hughes concocts a human (body) comedy that is hilarious, poignant, relentless, indelible. In the MTV-style montage of *Sixteen Candles* his camera focuses on teen hands slipped inside each other's patched jean pockets or linked by bent pinkies (a fad that must have lasted ten minutes). Repeatedly, bony boy hands twist a locker padlock, the metal door stubbornly shut–till the locker springs open and all manner of junk topples onto the unseen teen. And onto the audience, who may find a jammed-shut, crammed-full locker of their own high school memories tumbling out.

As the Geek in *Sixteen Candles*, Anthony Michael Hall knocks over the elaborately stacked beer cans of a jock posse and an enormous pile of metal car parts in a shop class. When the Geek gets his big chance to dance with Molly, when he flails before her in oblivious epileptic ecstacy, I wince for all of us who dared step onto an '80s dance floor. Gone was the safety of a shuffling bear-hug slow dance; gone were the anything-goes hippie-dippy moves and grooves of the '70s. The '80s demanded that teens vogue like Madonna.

My Geek was a senior nicknamed Squirm. I can't remember his real name. But Squirm–kindly, I know in retrospect–asked me to his prom. When he stood before me on the dance floor and, well, squirmed, I froze in horror like Molly in *Sixteen Candles* but did not, like her, let loose a shrill, satisfying scream.

In Hughes's cruel yet compassionate high school world even the Geek in *Sixteen Candles* eventually gets his due. When he finds himself with the prom queen in the morning, she tells him that she liked waking up in his arms. And the Geek, holding out those pencil-thin arms, asks incredulously: "*These* things?"

A girl in a neck brace, a running sight gag in *Sixteen Candles*, is also the film's most sympathetic character as she valiantly struggles to perform such normal yet impossible tasks as drinking from a hallway water fountain or, at the film's blowout party, sipping a beer. My Geek, on prom night, got sick on peppermint schnapps. True to '80s excess, Hughes uses a dizzying array of intoxicants to highlight such haplessness in both the geeky and the gorgeous.

The dead-drunk prom princess in *Sixteen Candles* gets her lush hair slammed in a door and consents to let her equally drunken girlfriends chop it off. In the comic climax Molly Ringwald's glamorous, uptight sister faces her wedding day high on an overdose of menstrual-cramp muscle relaxants. Rubber-limbed and -faced, she lurches her way down the aisle, biting her veil like cotton candy, shoving aside guests, and curling up on a pew like a baby.

5. "Excuse me for being a virgin"
So pleads Anthony Michael Hall as *The Breakfast Club*'s geek when he's pressured into publicly declaring whether he's had sex or not.

For John Hughes twists his dials highest not only on the most private bodily dysfunctions, but on—witness the Geek displaying Molly's panties to a pay-per-view bathroomful of boys—the most public possible humiliations. Ever prescient, predating the era of celebrity humiliation, John Hughes makes public humiliations a centerpiece of his teen universe. Of course, public humiliation of teens has existed ever since teens were first herded together.

But by the '80s new levels of shock were needed to register on the Richter scale of disgrace. As my husband observed, in the '60s all teens had to do to shock anyone was grow their hair long. In my '80s high school, jocks used the intercom system to announce—when scheduling a yearbook photo by the flagpole for the Thespians—that "all lesbians" gather round the "fag pole."

In Hughes's high-tech high school halls troops of geeks use telescopic glasses to spy on Molly; the ringleader geek worries that an imagined sex video of him and Molly will find its way onto the Net. Nice-girl Molly doesn't hesitate to announce to the Geek that he is "a total fag." And Molly herself is publicly derided by a rich boy in *Pretty in Pink* as "low-grade ass."

In *The Breakfast Club* a bad boy sprawls under Molly's desk and shoves his head up her skirt, between her legs. In *Sixteen Candles*, Molly is felt up by her mortifyingly uninhibited grandma ("Fred, she's gotten her boobies!" she squeals to the lecherous grandpa). This same Molly is horrified to learn that a sex test she filled out (penning earnest answers to such questions as "Have you ever touched it?") has fallen into the hands of her dream boy.

How potent these early humiliations can be; how potent still is my desire for the revenge that I fantasized about for my own teen tormentors: public humiliation on a national scale. Someday, when I was a writer, I'd reveal the names of my tormentors, first and last names! The girl who arranged my first kiss, instructing the boy to kiss me, then instantly tell me, "Fuck you."

How I longed to tell her (Kim Parkins, BTW) the same, in print. How I would have relished, had I seen it back then, Molly Ringwald's *Pretty in Pink* triumph as she shows up the girls who scorned her, stealing the prom in her homemade dress. But why does she choose the rich boy who initially scorned her too over the funnier, sweeter boy who lives to love her?

How guilty I feel myself to recall how I once gazed frankly

across a classroom at a quiet boy I liked. When he began mocking my own gaze, sending it back at me in such a blatant, bug-eyed imitation that the boy sitting next to him giggled, I glared and looked away. I hated that boy after that. Only years later when the boy had come out as gay, when I read of his tragically young death from AIDS, did I realize with a pang that perhaps he had thought I, with my inexpert but in-earnest gaze, had been trying to humiliate him.

John Hughes catches the shame on both sides of such games. By the ends of his Molly movies his tormented teen characters glimpse not only one anothers' private parts, but their shared vulnerabilities.

6. "We're all pretty bizarre"

Amid so much vividly depicted clumsiness and cruelty, the few moments of grace that Hughes allows his creations come across all the more powerfully.

In Hughes's world, as in life, most transcendent teen moments are connected to creativity and music. My own single happy moment in high school took place in my art room as I tranced out over a painting and suddenly the teacher allowed a rare radio to be switched on. "Goodbye Yellow Brick Road." I remember my own surprise as I moved my paintbrush with the rhythm and realized: *I'm in school and I'm actually happy.*

Each of Hughes's Molly movies features his patented MTV-style montages: ecstatic, poetic pastiches. Rapidly intercut high school images are arrayed to the beat of Hughes's dynamic sound tracks. The Psychedelic Furs growling "Pretty in Pink"; the Vapors manically "Turning Japanese." With his dead-on instincts, Hughes chooses songs that turn out to be *the* radio songs playing as his films open.

The Breakfast Club, arguably Hughes's most fully realized teen portrait, opens with David Bowie's "Changes" and a Bowie quote emblazoned on-screen about the children who are "spit on." In his striking *Breakfast Club* montage Hughes juxtaposes shots of a neat, hand-lettered cheerleader sign proclaiming SENIOR SPIRIT SOARS with scrawled graffiti that claims I'M EATING MY HEAD.

Compared with Hughes's other teen flicks, *The Breakfast Club* is both darker (in this one the parents are threatening rather than merely embarrassing) and more hopeful (with its final near-fantasy vision of geeks, head cases, bad boys, and prom queens all coming together, if only for a day).

In my senior year I found myself "in" at last, albeit with outsiders. So in *The Breakfast Club*, I relive my own Thespian Club community of misfits.

Lovingly portrayed by then-fresh Brat Pack faces (including Ally Sheedy as the dark-haired, thin-lipped tormented intellectual counterpart to Molly Ringwald's golden girl), Hughes's characters, trapped together in day-long detention, uncover one another's secrets and souls. A compact one-act play of a script puts the young stars through an emotional striptease. The good-guy jock (Emilio Estevez) confesses his own shame at his locker-room torment of a fellow wrestler; Molly Ringwald's princess mocks her own status ("I am so popular"); and Anthony Michael Hall's geek reveals his failed suicide attempt. And a galvanizing bad boy leads the group in defiant acts against their sadistic school ("Being bad," he tells Molly, "feels pretty good. Huh?").

The Brat Pack bonding climaxes with an exhilarating, no-holds-barred dance sequence. Each character, in his or her own distinctive way, cuts loose—the jock vaulting into handstands; the bad boy mock-boxing; the girls cancanning. We see and feel on-screen the real release of pent-up energy in their young bodies. By the improbable but moving finale the emotionally raw Breakfast Clubbers agree: "We're all pretty bizarre; some of us are just better at hiding it, that's all."

7. "You can't be sixteen forever"

Life after high school has not been easy for Molly Ringwald, at least on-screen. Her bad career karma seemed to begin when she turned down the lead in Hughes's *Some Kind of Wonderful.* As his next major romantic lead, Hughes cast Elizabeth McGovern in *She's Having a Baby.* For my money as a wife and mom, that film features one of film's more realistic–gross and gauzy at once–childbirth sequences. The film's young couple each feel they are married to a child, and an oldster grumbles at the yuppie duo's wedding: "People don't mature anymore. They stay jackasses all their lives."

Expanding his satirical reach to middle age, Hughes has cranked out raucous comedies starring eternally decadent John Candy. In *Uncle Buck,* Candy plays a charming man who seems to want to be a boy forever.

So in Hughes's film world, that fun-house mirror of our own, the adultized teens of the '80s have become the teenized adults of our times. But as Molly Ringwald noted wryly in an interview, "You can't be sixteen forever."

A friend of mine with a background in therapy likes to conduct an impromptu experiment: She instructs you to say the first thing that comes to your mind, then asks you, "How old are you?" The number that pops out of your mouth unbidden is, she claims, your "true age," the age you remain inside.

And the most common answer for middle-agers, she reports, is something in the teens. For me it was eighteen. Legally but not really an adult.

Maybe we whose primal screams were ringed with lip gloss

cling to our inner teen because we believe that deep down, as *The Breakfast Club* puts it, "when you grow up, your heart dies." For better or worse, John Hughes found our generation's heart. In his best films that eternally teenage heart still beats. And Molly Ringwald still screams for all of us, sixteen forever.

Make a Wish

THE FIRST KISS LASTS FOREVER

by Mary Sullivan

Where were you the morning John Lennon was shot?

I was curling my hair and applying gobs of blue eye shadow, getting ready for another hellish day in the life of a teenager. Something inside of me broke when the man on the radio said my favorite Beatle was dead, but I didn't put the curling iron down. I was dolling myself up, making another wish. Thinking today might be the day I fell in love, the day the fairy tale came true. I had to be ready. I had to Cinderellize myself.

I sang along, "'You say you want a revolution/Well you know . . .'"

The myth says that because Cinderella is good and beautiful and has the help of her fairy godmother, she overcomes her evil stepmother and stepsisters, then falls in love and marries the prince. Cinderella should get some credit here. It is only because she *acts* at all that she goes to the ball. But we all know the story. They live happily ever after. Justice is served and Cinderella finds her proper place in the world.

If anything, John Hughes is a believer in romantic love, ideal love, Cinderella love. The Cinderellas in his movies are good and true, unaware of their own beauty. But in their struggle to find love (and Hughes's love wears many masks), they learn to believe in themselves. They *act*, and by doing so, they make their wishes come true. They get their princes. There is always some surreal, comic crisis out of which the truth emerges, where we learn who is good and who is not. And music (the Beatles, the Stones, Simple Minds) is a catalyst for this magical, fairy-godmother moment, which inevitably leads to the transformation of our heroine into a princess. Love finds a home: a place to belong. Just as in the Cinderella story, Hughes's movies end with the happily-ever-after, the forever.

But let us start at the beginning.

The Conflict

In the fairy tale Cinderella, who is beautiful and good, weeps among the cinders because her evil stepmother makes her stay home and do all the work. Life is unfair.

In *Sixteen Candles*, Samantha Baker wakes up on her sixteenth birthday thinking her life is going to be transformed. It turns out to be the single worst day of her life, which begins with her parents (and the rest of her family) forgetting it's her birthday. Good, hardworking Andie Walsh, who wants only a date to the prom in *Pretty in Pink*, acts like more of a parent to her unemployed father than he does to her. In *The Breakfast Club* the five who meet at Sherman High detention have one thing in common: unsatisfactory family lives. The basket case's parents "ignore" her. The athlete says, "God, I fucking hate him! . . . He's like this mindless machine that I can't even relate to anymore." The brain is expected to be a genius. The princess is accused of having a "poor rich, drunk mother in the Caribbean," and the criminal's old man gave him a carton of cigarettes for Christmas.

Keith's father in *Some Kind of Wonderful* doesn't recognize the artist in his son. He expects Keith to go to college and be the first in his family who doesn't have to wash his hands after a day's work.

When Keith complains to his best friend, Watts, she says at least he has someone who cares. Her parents are completely absent. Ferris Bueller's parents don't want to know Ferris is taking the day off school. They are preoccupied to the point of being blind in *Ferris Bueller's Day Off*. Hughes's parents just don't get it. They are forgetful, busy, uncaring, shallow, overbearing, in denial, or just not there. All of them are fools.

In the '80s, John Hughes's movies saved us teenagers from loneliness, a desperate feeling of being unloved, unpretty, unrich, of being an *unperson*. He gave us a place to escape.

When I was growing up, if boys called, my father screened the calls. When one boy, Richie Bonano, called, my father called him Dicky Banana and told him to call back in fifteen years. At supper my father regularly lectured us (all eleven of us) on premarital sex, drugs, rock music, violence, etc. Hollywood was in great part to blame for this moral decline. The tradition of "family" was disintegrating, he told us. Just look at the divorce rate, blah, blah, blah. We shut our ears and finished our supper, and my mother quietly cleared the table.

And I dreamed of having a movie-star body, of wearing clothes that weren't hand-me-downs or from the church donation box, of going out with a boy who would save me from this unfair world. Who would take me to the movies and parties with loud music and kiss me. Forever.

The Invitation

An invitation arrives from the prince that says all the ladies in the land are invited to the ball. In an egalitarian world this includes Cinderella.

In study hall in *Sixteen Candles*, Samantha answers the "Sex Test" question "With who? (Be honest, your name's not on this, so it's okay)" by writing the name of her crush, Jake Ryan. She drops the test over her shoulder to her best friend, but Jake snags it. The "Sex Test" turns out to be Samantha's invitation into Jake's world. Jake asks his friend, with whom he's doing pull-ups at the gym, if he'd ever go out with Samantha Baker. "Depends on how much you paid me," the friend says. Jake responds, "She's not ugly." The friend says of Sam, who is not in the in-crowd, "It's not ugly, it's just . . . void." Samantha's prince says, "She looks at me like she's in love with me."

If the brain, the athlete, the basket case, the princess, and the criminal hadn't met that Saturday morning for detention, they would never have spoken, much less felt invited to reveal a single truth to one another. The moment they come together, they stop being afraid and share their secrets. The basket case is there because she "didn't have anything better to do." But she went; she did *something*. The prince never knew Cinderella existed until he saw her at the ball. Until she *acted*.

Pretty in Pink centers on Andie's getting a date to the prom with rich and popular Blane. In *Some Kind of Wonderful*, Keith doesn't see his Cinderella is right there beside him, until Watts chaperones him on his fantasy date. The two nerds in *Weird Science*, Gary and Wyatt, write their own invitation on a computer program to create the ideal woman. Little do they know she will be *real*.

My invitation came when I sneaked to a party and met *him* the first time. It wasn't only that he was a senior dating a cheerleader and he played the guitar, went to rock concerts, and had his own car (even if it was a Le Car). It was that when I looked at him, I saw myself as I wanted to be. When he asked me if I was going to the talent show, my heart skipped a beat.

Then my baneful older sister, knowing I had sneaked out, showed up at the party with the news that my father was outside waiting for me. I ran to the bathroom to hide. Because there was no toothpaste to take away the smell of beer in my mouth, I bit into a bar of soap. My father wasn't there at all, but I went home out of shame.

A tenth grader, I knew nothing of love except that I wanted it, that I believed in it, and that it was open to everyone, as Cinderella proved.

The Obstacles

When Cinderella is told she can't go to the ball, she runs outside in her tattered rags and cries. Her stepmother and stepsisters go.

Samantha Baker has chosen Jake as her ideal even though he has a girlfriend who is popular and rich and has the perfect body. The camera caresses her as she showers in the girls' locker room. Sam tells herself that she "needs four inches of bod." And she decides to go to the school dance that night though Long Duk Dong, the foreign exchange student staying with her family, is accompanying her.

As is the case in many of John Hughes's movies, our heroine isn't rich or popular enough for her prince. Though she has an inner beauty and goodness, she's on the wrong side of the tracks, and she suffers for this. In *Pretty in Pink*, Blane's friend says of Andie, "If you got a hard-on for trash, don't take care of it around us, pal." While Keith's dream date, Amanda Jones, "runs with the rich and the beautiful," Watts wears men's underwear and dog tags. Just as Cinderella's beauty is masked in rags, Watts hides in her black leather coat and tough-girl looks. The only way Watts can get in on the Cinderella date is to dress up as chaperone for the fairy-tale couple.

At first all the social and class differences between the brain, the basket case, the criminal, the athlete, and the princess create walls between them, keeping them from seeing themselves as individuals. They, too, are trapped by the stereotypes that define them. In the gimmicky *Weird Science*, when Lisa is simulated into being, not only is she a babe, but she has a brain. She is a real person, and Gary and Wyatt don't know what to do with her, much less how to hide her from Chet, Wyatt's evil brother.

I had to contend with my father, who was in love with making rules: no sleepovers, no TV, no movies, no drinking, no being alone with the opposite sex in any room in our house (including my sister and her fiancé, both in their late twenties), no drugs, no bikinis, no staying out past ten. And at every pep rally and basketball game I had to watch my crush's girlfriend shaking her pom-poms, her blue and white pleated skirt floating up with each jump to reveal long, perfect legs. Worse, she sat one row over in Spanish class. I pretended I didn't hear her and her friends whispering or see them glaring at me. Clearly, I was heading into dangerous territory, namely theirs. My stomach hurt. I escaped to the school nurse.

A Little Bit of Magic
Cinderella's fairy godmother gives her a gown, glass slippers, and a coach with horses and a footman to go to the ball.

Love is more powerful than magic, but for John Hughes teenage love *needs* a little magic–often a little *Midsummer Night's Dream* magic. It seems this crazed drama where the world turns upside down is necessary somehow to restore proper order. Only then do our heroines stop being afraid that who they are isn't enough.

In *Sixteen Candles*, in the auto shop the night of the school dance, Sam tells the Geek, "Well, I can't get happy. It is physically impossible for me to get happy." She can't get happy until she learns Jake was asking about her. Later that night while a high school party is raging in full-on drunken madness at Jake's house, the camera cuts between Jake and Sam, both lying awake and alone, thinking of the other. All the while love is brewing.

In *The Breakfast Club* and *Some Kind of Wonderful* the magic is internal. Light works its way outward, into the characters' Cinderella eyes, and a glow spreads over their faces. At the start, the basket case sits in the back of the detention room dressed in black, taking turns hiding in her coat, biting her nails and spitting them out, and scratching dandruff onto the desk where she is sketching a scene with snow. She is transformed when the princess-turned-fairy-godmother makes her over.

Hair pulled back in a white ribbon and dressed in a lacy blouse, the basket case–turned–true-princess walks toward the athlete. Her eyes are bright and her face is radiant. He steps toward her. "What happened to you?" The music plays–always the music–pulling us in, screaming out, daring us. He says, "I can see your face."

The moment before Watts practice-kisses Keith to prepare him for his dream date, her eyes flutter, her mouth opens slightly, and she swallows her breath. When his lips touch hers, glass shatters in the background and music breaks through. The song goes like this: "The first kiss lasts forever. She loves me." This is magic.

I couldn't go anywhere, my father saw to that, but I could go to a school function. The night of the talent show the moon was a huge white ball. Something in the air made my skin soft and tingly. Something electrical. Something so pure no one could see it. I was in the audience when my prince played Neil Young's "Sugar Mountain" on acoustic guitar.

I had to be home way before midnight, but even then, at that early hour, I knew the magic couldn't last. Or my secret would be revealed and my prince would know I was terrified. Of love–without the magic.

The Prince Falls in Love

Cinderella goes to the ball and the prince falls in love with her.
When the clock strikes midnight, however, the magic runs out.
Cinderella loses her power and her gown turns to rags.

Jake and Samantha never actually dance, but as often happens with high school love, there is a mediator (the Geek) to communicate what the other is thinking. This isn't about sex, either, but about love and longing. Jake wants someone real he can fall in love with, not the void of his dippy girlfriend.

In *The Breakfast Club* each confesses a truth, and it is the truth that binds the five, if only for that single day in March. On this day they dance and laugh and cry together, transcending the stereotypes cast upon them. They become "quite aware of what they're going through." As they understand one another, they break through the chains society has imposed upon them, and the athlete kisses the basket case, the criminal kisses the princess, and the brain kisses the essay he wrote for Mr. Vernon–happy at last. For Hughes, only teenagers are open-minded enough to believe wholly in new possibilities and new love.

In *Some Kind of Wonderful* the camera arcs around the lovers (who don't yet know they are lovers) as they practice-kiss. Watts wraps her legs around Keith, pulling him to her, unable to hide herself in the kiss. But she is not Amanda Jones.

My life was never the same after my first real kiss. He gave me a ride home from the talent show in his Le Car. We parked under a juniper tree with the moon above us. The Beatles were playing. When he kissed me, I knew that first kiss would last forever. There is nothing like first love.

I made my wish and then, before the magic could end, I dashed out of the Le Car. If he saw who I really was, he might change his mind. He might wish I were someone else. He would see that I

wasn't quite tall or thin enough, that there was a stain on the right
sleeve of my shirt, that my sandals, a size too big, kept slipping off
my feet. As much as I wanted the dream, I was sure it would dis-
appear when the magic did.

Everyone Must Try On the Slipper (Except Cinderella)

*The prince's messenger goes to every house in the land with the
glass slipper for everyone to try on. Cinderella's stepmother and
stepsisters laugh at her when she suggests she try on the slipper. But
as we know, justice is served.*

The magic is over, but the truth has been revealed in the shape
of a missing glass slipper: the proof in the pudding, the evidence
that love indeed existed. Hughes's movies are about romantic love,
but also about how one finds her place in the world. His Cinderellas
find their places in the unhappy world of high school, and when
they do, they discover their true selves.

After Sam's sister, Ginny, has married her cad of a husband, the
wedding party abandons Sam on the church steps. Across the street
Jake is leaning against his car. When he waves, Sam looks behind
her to see if someone is there. She points to herself in her "dipshit"
pretty-princess bridesmaid dress. "Yeah, you," Jake says. He jogs to
her, sweeps her off her feet, and gallops her away (in his car) to his
parents' house.

In *Pretty in Pink*, Andie designs and sews what is supposed to
be a stunningly beautiful pink prom dress. It fits her like a glass slipper. In *Weird Science*, where love is instant, Wyatt and Gary learn
from their fantasy woman, Lisa, that people "will like you for what
you are, not for what you can give them." Furthermore, Chet is
turned into a fat, troll-like creature who Lisa demands must treat
Wyatt and Gary with dignity and respect, just as Cinderella's stepsisters must treat her—after the slipper fits.

In *The Breakfast Club* the basket case and the athlete kiss in the parking lot while Simple Minds sing, "Don't don't don't don't don't you forget about me. . . ." She rips a patch off his jacket before she gets into her car. We don't know if any of the five will talk to one another in school on Monday, but the moment they all march out of Sherman High together, they are equals. They are in this–this trial of teenage life–together.

On the night of the *Some Kind of Wonderful* dream date, Hughes juxtaposes images of Amanda Jones and Watts showering, fixing their hair, putting on earrings, and applying makeup. Dressed in a chauffeur hat, coat, and gloves, Watts drives Amanda and Keith in a rented Jaguar. She is the Cinderella on the outside looking in, waiting for the slipper.

I didn't have a record player, but my prince took me to Strawberries and bought me my first record, Bob Dylan's *Shot of Love*, a Special Savers. I went home and wrote my first name and his last name in print, in cursive, in capital letters. There was nothing my father could do. The glass slipper fit.

They Live Happily Ever After
Cinderella and the prince marry and live happily ever after in his castle. Love is fulfilled.

In the final shot of *Sixteen Candles*, Jake says, "Happy birthday, Samantha. Make a wish," to which Sam says, "It already came true." A birthday cake between them, they smile at each other, then very slowly lean forward and kiss. Dreams do come true.

Andie, in her god-awful pretty-in-pink dress, not only gets Blane at the prom, but they confess their love for each other. Wyatt and Gary remain true to themselves *and* get the cool, popular girls in *Weird Science*.

In something of a twist of plot Amanda Jones turns out to be some kind of wonderful girlfriend. Of the diamond earrings Keith gives her, she says, "In your heart you wanted to give these to somebody else." Only then does Keith realize who the true Cinderella of his dreams is. He remembers the practice kiss, then runs down the street, picks Watts up, and spins her around, kissing her under glowing balls of streetlights. When he gives her the diamond earrings, she says, "I wanted these. I really wanted them."

As for me, he loved me. He really did. He was my one and only. That should have been where my movie ended. Then I could say with complete conviction: See, as in teenage dreams, Hughes movies follow the Cinderella plot.

But the films never show the happily-ever-after, where life becomes tricky. I never married my high school prince. He never swept me away in his Le Car forever after. But he still shows up regularly in my dreams. And when I watch John Hughes movies now, I become a teenager again. I believe in first love, true love, that Cinderella love, that John Hughes love. I do. I tell myself that the basket case is wrong when she says, "When you grow up, your heart dies." And I tell myself maybe, just maybe, I'll find my high school prince again. Might require a revolution. Might be in heaven. Might be a whole other kind of movie.

For now I'm still singing:

"Well you know
You better free your mind instead

. . . .

Don't you know it's gonna be all right
All right . . ."

In What Way Does the Author's Use of the Prison Symbolize...?

A DEEP EGO-IDENTIFICATION WITH FERRIS BUELLER

by Rebecca Wolff

In 2005 I attended my twentieth high school reunion and got to be the One No One Thought Would Show Up. I was approached and saluted, as I had been in high school itself, with caution and awkward admiration. But at the thronged nightclub, where the DJ reinforced a disorienting sense of collective mortality by playing deep cuts from the '80s, songs we hadn't heard since last we held boom boxes on our laps–"Set it off on the left, y'all / Set it off on the right, y'all"–I surprised everyone, including myself, with how uncontrollably pleased I was to see all the assorted coconuts. I smiled and nodded at folks I had never given the time of day in the dim hallways: the perky newscaster's daughter, now in the biz herself, who was *thrilled!* to find out that we both had two children, and therefore, presumably, something to talk about; the obeisant, balding man, known in his wiry youth as God's Favorite for his rumored ability to pleasure himself orally, who now dwelt somewhere deep inside the corporate structure; the lesbian photojournalist who had been the rosy-faced girl who snapped a shot of me and my best friend for the yearbook in our impossibly cool garb and our freakishly cool pose, and who snapped a shot of us now and wondered if we had always known she was gay (we hadn't–we were too busy pretending we were); the teeming hordes–long-haired Orthodox girl from homeroom, Indian boy who ran our school's government–whose names I'd never known but whose faces rose before me like miniature moons on the dark dance floor, where no one danced and I eventually waded to the turntables to request not a song, but that the volume be turned down so that we could all stop shouting at one another, like the middle-aged former club kid I am. The reunion proceeded, in fact, a lot like a scene from a John Hughes movie, one of those montages where he manages to accurately capture, in a panoramic view with clever editing and sunspot close-ups, the exact tenor of a group experience.

The first time I watched Ferris Bueller take his day off, I was at a drive-in movie theater in the deep summertime, a year or so out of high school and well into a hallucinogen-induced anxiety disorder, and I don't remember anything else about it. I believe I may have wondered why they chose such a dorky name for the character if he was supposed to be so cool. And what the hell city that was supposed to be; it certainly wasn't my city, with everyone driving around in cars. In my city you took the subway.

The first time I watched the film as an adult, I felt a jolt of recognition: Here, finally, was a teenage hero I could, with hindsight, relate to my own teenage self. No sad-sack, freckled Molly, no grinning, tighty-whitey Tom; here was one for whom everything fell beautifully into place, as it had, for a time, for me. Ferris manifests– principally, radically–all the positive and negative qualities I was credited with by those who reported back to me: infallibility, unflappableness, will bordering on amorality, antiauthoritarianism bordering on self-rule. The whole movie is about him cutting a day of school, for chrissakes; it *still* makes me feel cool to relate that I absented myself from the entire spring of my senior year. Never mind that I spent many of those spring days in the office of a wizened

Austrian psychotherapist and the balance sitting in my living room in front of the dark television, afraid to turn it on, afraid of what I might be afraid of.

You can tell Ferris is cool by the posters in his room (and here I refer to the Internet, where you can immerse yourself in numerous sites devoted to Ferris trivia) (if you're a huge dork): Simple Minds, the Damned, Cabaret Voltaire. From my current vantage point, wherein teenage cool is obscured by the decades and, for all I know, consists in chastity and love of a Christian God, Ferris looks about right. Matthew Broderick is unchangeably clean-cut and sweet looking; even when he's doing Really Bad Stuff, like being unforgivably snotty to a restaurant employee (let's not even go into the class claustrophobia implicit in this film) (or let's: Ferris and friends are white, wealthy, suburban, and privileged, and lampoon/mistrust/objectify anyone who is not), he is doing it in the guise of a moneyed, upstanding citizen, rather than that of some scruffy street tough like Charlie Sheen's nameless ruffian, the guy I would definitely have fucked in the bathroom of the police station, if I were Jennifer Grey before her career-occluding nose job.

Ferris is a special kind of cool, though: He is cool in the way that God is cool. He is so cool that all his scheming, all his machinations, all his cruelty to his best friend, Cameron—whom he dominates, exploits, and subjects to the sight of constant PDA with his perfect girlfriend, Sloane, with whom he is clearly having sex—turn out in the end to be in the service of Cameron's well-being. Ferris works in mysterious ways. As the adoring, exquisitely smutty Sloane muses rhetorically (at least in the film, if not in the original script), "You knew what you were doing when you woke up this morning, didn't you?" In the end, we are to understand, Ferris has orchestrated this whole day off around the pressing psychic needs of his best friend.

Is Ferris a god, that he is so wise, so fully realized, so machina? Or is he a figment? If this film were a dream, then Cameron would be the dreamer and Ferris the better part of his shattered psyche. Ferris is a totality in the midst of parts; Ferris, it seems, will never get his comeuppance. Indeed, Ferris's one tremor of fallibility is the catalyst for what I would bet good money is the film's true denouement, chase scene or no. After a long day's journey into the heart of downtown 1986 Chicago, where the bloom is not yet off the lip-synching rose and all the missing black people come out, dancing, from behind a rock, Ferris finds that he is unable to turn back the hands of time (Cameron's dad's Ferrari's odometer). This miscalculation leads to Cameron's becoming the true hero of the film, relegating Ferris to the, after all, cooler status of antihero. Because the odometer will not turn back, Cameron must face up to his father–and his resentment of, domination by, same. Thus Ferris has forced his best friend, with brutal invasiveness, to confront his demons. Cameron will not be allowed to venture forth in life a spiritual and emotional cripple. It's an intervention! Cameron, with his squinty, bedazzled eyes, lantern jaw, and slitty, Republican-style lips, must self-actualize!

Self-revelation is purported to be–perhaps demonstrated to be–the first step in self-actualization. Cameron will never escape his agonized, constrained condition without the burst of speech that prefaces his fateful kicking of his dad's Ferrari's bumper. I myself have waited twenty years for the appropriate venue to arise in which to go into great depth about how cool I was in high school. I've begun (and abandoned) poems about my coolness, dropped (neglected) conversational prompts, attempted to use it as a divisive tool–a wedge, that is–in my relationship with my husband, who was an Ultimate Frisbee player in high school (a very special, lanky kind of nerd). I've discussed the fallout of my coolness in therapy. I've hashed over the characteristics of my coolness with the several friends who linger from that time—my intimidating presence, my unflappable sheen. I've stepped back from myself—even further back—countless times and tried a calculation of the parts that made that particular whole: physical authority—a certain louche, deliberate way of walking and speaking; my heavy mouth, which falls into a sneer when at rest; an experimental approach to hair color and makeup that coincided brilliantly with the advent of New Wave; my willingness to experiment also with mind-altering substances, which seemed like a natural response to the early 1980s in New York City.

Most often, though, the subject comes up in the context of a negation: No, I was not a loser in high school, like all the other poets. I have felt it very keenly that this be understood, as there is a general assumption that those who become poets must all have run the same painful gantlet of exclusion, uncertainty, embarrassment, loneliness. High school was not, as a different kind of loser is known to allege it to be, the best four years of my life, thank God, but neither was it an endless parade of misery, a long, fluorescently lit hallway of insult and rejection, a demoralizing succession of shames and exclusions. Rather, for whatever panoply of reasons, whatever agglomeration of conditions, I was a particular kind of winner: in demand as a companion, gazed on from afar by those not lucky enough to come closer. I received, no joke, daily compliments on my appearance and manner. I was objectified, I was fetishized.

I was not, however, one of those teenagers that adults recognize as being *truly* cool—the sweet, often quiet kids who have no need for attention-getting antics or hair dye or piercings, who rest easily on the social ladder, who possess a sturdy, lasting confidence that will keep them from ever getting into any real trouble, who are centered and curious and nice to everyone and loved by everyone, and who will have deep relationships with their grateful parents throughout their long lives. No, I was imbalanced, and unprepared, and acutely conscious of this dark dominion of mine. I guarded it carefully. By no means was I nice to everyone. I would not be seen talking to some science dork, some awkward weirdo, some ugly girl with stupid clothes. Or even a pretty girl with stupid clothes. I remember the strange feeling that came over me when I did, by happenstance, bounce up against a kid like this: a normal kid, a "straight" kid—we used this term before it meant, exclusively, "heterosexual." Though I was never intentionally mean, there was, rather, a panicky delicacy that arose as I tried to get out of his or her conversational range as quickly as possible. I was the kind of teenager that, however inadvertently, makes other teenagers feel bad. Thus this revelation turns out to be not one of coolness, but of its failure.

My own episode of fallibility was not so handy, nor so benevolent, as Ferris's. What I think of, in my more karmically inclined moments, as a comeuppance took the form, in the spring of my senior year of high school, of a nasty acid trip, one of those whoppers you hear about, the ones that last for years, that turn the sufferer into a basket case—seeing things that are not there and fearing things that are not real. This was a hammerlike hit of acid that split open all the flaws in the facets of my cultivated gem of a personality, revealing negative traits in inverse correlation to what had appeared on the surface: social anxiety of a pervasive, mushroom-cloud-like insidiousness; existential doubt to rival that of Kierkegaard; paranoid susceptibility to basic insecurities of all sorts. I was a quivering mass of jelly, and no one could help me. Few, in fact, understood what was happening to me, as I was practically mute, practically immobilized, could not articulate or gesticulate anything about the horrific interior experience of my dark days and nights. Of the early days—it went on for years—I remember best one bright spring Saturday morning when two friends came to my house (my apartment, that is; no one lived in a "house") to try to draw me outside. I would go only as far as the stoop, and sat with them there, not saying much, struggling to keep myself from moaning out loud. I was not really there; I was removed from the moment and the human presences of my friends as if by a wedge. It felt permanent, and deeply painful. My mother came along and took photographs of us, and this is the only reason I remember the day, the only reason I can believe that I was smiling shyly, with my bleached-blond hair, embraced on both sides by my friends.

Ferris Bueller's day off is a little bit like a dream: It is a wish fulfillment, in which Ferris "gets away with it." It is illogical like a dream: Oh, sure, Ferris could really figure out exactly how to program, or jerry-rig, his doorbell, his answering machine. Sure his dad wouldn't recognize his only son in a taxicab next to him in a traffic jam. Oh, sure. And, as in a dream, all the film's characters can be seen to represent different facets of the dreamer's self, the protoganist's self, the viewer's self—or the director's self, if you want to take the auteur route. I prefer to take the "I contain multitudes" route and to think of Ferris's day off in terms of a free play of the psyche (my psyche, that is) across the field of ego-relatedness. I am the dreamer, and Ferris and Cameron and Sloane and Jeanie and the unnamed ruffian are avatars of various aspects of Self, desirable and not so. Cameron is the damaged Self, the one who needs healing. Sloane is a figure of capitulation: She will accompany, she will reinforce, she will buffer, she will marry. (She will have little dialogue.) Jeanie is the site of self-loathing, of misdirected anger, of that which needs to get laid. Ferris, of course, represents what I'd like to recall for you—and for myself—in myself: the most superficial, most pleasurable, least enduring perfection. All my posturing, past and present, comes down to a homely gratitude for my moments in the sun. While the comeuppance, and the comedown, were hard, I imagine that it would have really sucked to be a loser.

Just joking.

Ferris, of course, represents the Self that is in dialogue with the Other, the Self that transcends and thereby actualizes, Selfhood–that intercedes on the other's behalf. Notably, in Ferris's world (i.e., his high school) there aren't any real losers. Rather, the underclass of the school are merely younger, less experienced, in need of Ferris's help. He is their Bad Daddy, their "righteous dude," getting them out of summer school, and they repay him with good wishes, even a pornographic singing telegram.

I often think back to a girl whose name I never knew. She was in my grade. She was tall and gawky and had unruly hair cut in a style that would be all the rage in 2005, but she couldn't possibly have known that. It was sort of Rod Stewartish. She wore octagonal granny glasses. She almost always wore a crocheted sweater vest, in the style of an afghan, which looked distinctly homemade. She wore no makeup. She looked, in short, as though she had been dressed by her hippie mother, and this suspicion was reinforced by the fact that her younger sister attended our high school as well and was dressed similarly. Most memorably, though, she did not look miserable. She looked smart, and sharp, and sophisticated in some way that I could not name, a sort of tomboyish, absentminded-professorish cool imported from another rubric, another matrix, a set of rules I didn't have access to. I have always wished that I had been the kind of teenager who would have been friends with this girl and had a good time doing some unimaginable things with her–perhaps talking about our favorite books. I looked around for her at the reunion, but she had decided to stay home. Or perhaps she's dead.

How John Hughes Altered My Life

by Moon Unit Zappa

I am thirteen. My class goes on a sleepover field trip to spend five days in the Marin headlands observing marine life up close. When we arrive, the boys and girls are divided between two beige rectangular buildings that smell like seaweed, mildew, and almond-scented soap. I take a lower bunk in the squelchy girls' dormitory and settle in. I unroll my sleeping bag in my cubby, lie on my back, and un-Velcro my magenta '80s ripper wallet to remove the magazine tear-out I stole out of a *GQ* magazine at my best friend's house. I unfold the glossy men's quarterly image for the four hundredth time, see the dark-haired boy with the crew cut, shirtless and lithe from water sports, if you are willing to believe what you see in the photo (I am), and tape him near the knots and whorls of the wooden ceiling of my bunk bed. My friends all wish they had brought something from home to decorate their beds.

During the day I carry the male model around in a waterproof plastic pencil bag as we hike along coastal ridges, watch whales migrate, and study tide pools teeming with life. At night he is safely tucked in my back pocket as we watch slide shows about pollution and its impact on the environment, marvel at how protozoan-inhabited ocean water lights up Day-Glo green when stirred and viewed in the dark, then rally around a campfire to sing jingoistic school songs and to stargaze. Later the popular girls sneak off and kiss the popular boys, but not me. I am not popular. I am jealous, but I am not lonely. I have him.

When they say lights-out, I kiss my finger, then use the same finger to touch the male model's paper-creased cheek before closing my eyes for sleep.

When I get home to Hollywood, California, I am tan and tired. I ask our housekeeper to make me a quesadilla, which I slothfully eat in front of the TV. I see a trailer for a movie that stars the dark-haired puppy-love obsession of mine. I rally and make my mother drive me to the newsstand so I can buy a *Tiger Beat* magazine and read up on the latest "news." The facts I commit to memory are this: The boy I love is named Michael Schoeffling. He is much older than I am, around twenty. He will star in a movie called *Sixteen Candles* opposite a pouty-lipped, redheaded girl named Molly Ringwald. A man named John Hughes discovered them. Molly Ringwald is John Hughes's muse. John Hughes taped a photo of this girl above his desk and wrote the entire movie for her and has already written another film with her in mind.

I look up the word "muse" in our big dictionary. It means "to think about something in a deep and serious or dreamy and abstracted way." I read about Michael Schoeffling over and over again. I decide this handsome older boy is my muse. If I ever get to meet him, I will surely die. I have no idea how to pronounce his last name.

Growing up the daughter of a sixties rock icon was pretty much what one might imagine: I was offered a diaphragm at age twelve and was told that when I had sleepovers, I had to shower with whomever I was dating so we could save water. My rock royalty of a dad toured for nine months out of the year, cheated on my mom when he was away, but always came home to us, to sleep all day and work all night.

Normal to me was parents who slept in the nude and had loud sex while I tried to sleep one room over. Normal to me was leaving frozen meat out on the pancake grill to thaw, and if the cats still nibbled on the end of the bloody paper a few days later, the meat was still good enough to cook. Normal to me was having a "fan" (generally a freaky nuthouse escapee or similar) ringing our doorbell at all hours to harass my father or offer us the gift of homemade yogurt kept in an old pool chlorine container and stored under the floorboards of their basement or a dirty sleeping bag. Normal to me was wearing my ruffly underwear on my head like a hat and hitchhiking with my barefoot mother to the canyon store for peanut butter and milk. Normal to me was definitely *not* John Hughes's safe-as-houses Illinois suburbs populated by sweet-natured misfits and his archetypal portraits of the American family.

At our house everything was out in the open, including the brutality and instability of the nuclear age we were living in and my parents' struggling-artist finances. Sure, we could curse as much as we wanted, stay up until all hours watching R-rated TV or porn, drink or do drugs (so long as we did it at home . . . so why bother), but we were not allowed to do common, everyday things like get a job. Showing up at the same location at the same time meant someone might be watching you, like a murderer, so if I took walks in my neighborhood, I was taught to stagger the departure hour, destination, and duration to throw kidnappers and rapists off my scent. Maybe it's because my father was thrown off the stage by a "fan" and was in a body cast for almost a year, but for as modern and unconventional a household as I was raised in, we ever-so-fun Zappas were 100 percent sheltered.

I am fourteen. During the day I am an acne-ridden freshman struggling to get by at a hippie prep school. At night I make my dad laugh by impersonating my female classmates or the girls I've overheard talking at the mall or at the umpteen bar/bat mitzvahs I have attended. Always I carry around the handsome stranger in my pant pocket like a talisman fending off the torture of adolescent hormone spikes and boredom.

One evening my father wakes me up in the dead of night on a school night. He tells me he wants me to come downstairs to the recording studio and do the funny voice I do that he loves. I like the musty cigarette smell of his carpeted world, the different-colored lacquered woods of all the instruments, and the squishiness of the rubber on the headphones I wear in the quiet of the soundproof vocal booth.

My mic is adjusted and I record a song with my father called "Valley Girl." It will appear on my dad's album *Ship Arriving Too Late to Save a Drowning Witch*. When my father goes on tour a few weeks later, my mom is sad. To get us off her back and be alone with her depression for a few minutes, the ritual of taking me and my siblings to the movies begins. Over the years we see all the hits of the day: *Poltergeist, ET, Blade Runner, Tootsie, Flashdance, WarGames* . . . When *Sixteen Candles* finally rolls around, (which has since become my all-time favorite John Hughes movie) I am overjoyed.

At the local 250-seat theater with only one screen and one person behind the lone concession stand, all of us settled in with buttered popcorn, Dr Pepper, candied almonds, and chocolate-covered raisins, the lights go down. Within minutes I am stunned into helpless paroxysms of laughter, tears, and speechlessness. Not only do I see Jake Ryan (aka my lucky charm of a fantasy boyfriend) living, breathing, moving, and talking, but I see a world so foreign to me I may as well be watching *Star Wars* instead of *Sixteen Candles*; both are science fiction.

As I watch my monobrowed hottie chase after a girl he realizes he adores exactly *because* she is not like the popular girls he is supposed to like, I think, *What is this unknown land with customs and values I did not previously know I admired?* When I watch the father-daughter chat where a preoccupied grown-up apologizes for forgetting a neglected kid's birthday, I think, *No one ever talks to me about big feelings I might be experiencing while pubescent hormones make a war zone of my physiology, psychology, and physiognomy.*

Compared with my upbringing, the angst-laden teenage world I am viewing is almost banal, yet it is exactly this commonplaceness, this exotic pedestrianism, that I did not previously realize how desperately I craved. We certainly do not eat dinner as a family or celebrate fake moneymaking events like weddings or sweet sixteens. We never take family vacations and are never left alone with extended relatives like the rest of the entire planet I have no real interaction with. How come I didn't know happy, sane families existed, let alone imagine what one might look like? And why didn't anyone tell me how to have a proper crush or what to do about it if you caught one?

Sitting in the dark of the theater as the credits to this life-changing movie roll, I file these and other idealized personal and family awarenesses away, as with so many other firsts I will encounter through the long list of the jowly director's miraculous works.

Before John Hughes, growing up as I did, my plan was to have a bunch of kids and raise them without a man around, just like my foxy mom, only my brood would be sired by a bunch of different dads so that I could sleep around, just like my bitchin' father. Post–John Hughes my revised, scaled-down plan is to marry Michael Schoeffling, befriend Molly Ringwald, and become John Hughes's other muse.

• • •

I am fourteen and a half. The song I recorded with my father is an overnight hit. I am immediately thrust into the limelight. Since my father is touring overseas in Europe, I am forced to do press in the United States to promote the satirical collaboration. I appear on *Late Night with David Letterman, The Merv Griffin Show, Solid Gold,* and *Real People,* to name a few. As a result some casting agents take an interest and I get cast in a couple of movies. One of them is *European Vacation,* based on a story by John Hughes. Now I am sure I will become his other muse and, of course, marry Michael!

But Amy Heckerling, of *Fast Times at Ridgemont High* fame, will direct, so my two imaginary friends never pop by the set, and my life wearily trudges on without them.

I spend the next batch of my teenage days auditioning and booking more minor roles in film and television. It's 1985. By now I have seen and absolutely loved *The Breakfast Club,* but my commitment to Michael Schoeffling doesn't falter, so on weekends I go clubbing to try to meet him. There's just something primordial about his chocolate brown forever eyes. . . .

Since I am radically underage, club owners sneak me in the back, stamp my hand, and take me straight to the VIP room. Celebrities get everything on the house. I ask for a Coke, but cocaine is brought out instead. When I clarify and say, "Coca-Cola, please," the bartender doesn't miss a beat, only scoops shaved ice into a clear glass with one hand and squeezes the soda trigger with the other.

As my main prize continues to elude me by refusing to be at whatever hot spot I am haunting, I make up for it by meeting other beloved teen idols: Anthony Michael Hall, Tatum O'Neal, Brooke Shields, Janet Jackson, Kirk Cameron, Drew Barrymore, Christopher Atkins, Michael J. Fox, Emilio Estevez, Charlie Sheen, and Tom Cruise. L.A. is actually a small town, only instead of running into the local hardware store owner or greengrocer, it's Jodie Foster you meet or Matt Dillon and you make out with him in the dirty stairwell of a dingy dance club.

One summer evening I inadvertently come across Molly Ringwald. She is singing standards in a local nightclub with her blind father. She has a beautiful singing voice. I am impressed. We meet, and she and I have a lot in common besides appearing on the TV show *The Facts of Life*. Both our dads are musicians, we both like Lean Cuisine and the band Madness . . . but it's obvious to anyone Molly is a lot cooler than me. She has cool clothes and accessories, especially cool hats, she knows how to apply makeup, *and* she has boobs.

Once she lets me help her dye her hair while she sits on her family's diving board and enlightens me about Edie Sedgwick and Suzanne Vega. Another time she comes to my house for a sleepover, but she meets my brother Dweezil and decides to sleep in his room instead. Eventually they become boyfriend and girlfriend. He even gets a small part in *Pretty in Pink*. Maybe now I'll meet John Hughes and run off with Michael Schoeffling!

But John Hughes doesn't direct. Some balding guy who chews carrots with his mouth open does instead, and Michael isn't even considered for the cast. The pursuit is still on!

Only I am not sure what else I can do besides loiter in trendy bars, restaurants, and nightclubs from L.A. to New York that I read about in magazines.

I am seventeen. I am at Disneyland with Molly, my brother Dweezil, and a bunch of her friends. Molly is going to be featured in *Life* magazine. A journalist and a photographer are assigned to follow her around while a bunch of her best pals tag along. I wonder,

Are Michael Schoeffling and John Hughes considered friends or coworkers?

They never turn up, but at the Happiest Place on Earth, I still manage to have a good time. We go to the head of every line and ride our favorite rides before everyone else, and as many times as we want. When the journalist is done interviewing Molly, he questions us about her while the photographer snaps away. We eat hot dogs and Carnation milk, which I puke up right after we ride the Mad Tea Party teacups.

Even though I am clearly one of Molly's closest friends (why else would I be at Disneyland with her?), I am still way too shy to ask her anything about my future husband. Anyway, I don't want to be one of those awful people who take advantage and ask for creepy favors. I see how annoying it is to my famous dad. I suppose I could contact his agent, and say what? Can you please have him call me? No way, too desperate. I want to meet him on my terms. I'll leave it up to fate. Maybe I don't want to know if she slept with him.

A short time later it looks as if Molly and my brother might call it quits. Now I really can't say anything about M.S. When they break up, I choose my brother's feelings, so I get broken up with too.

I am nineteen. As much as I laugh watching *Weird Science, Some Kind of Wonderful,* and *Ferris Bueller's Day Off,* I am bummed John Hughes hasn't cast my dream man again. I try to watch Michael Schoeffling in *Belizaire the Cajun* and *Vision Quest,* but I can't care about period pieces or the boring old wrestling world. Some say M.S. is wooden, but they are wrong. He just isn't being given the right roles. Why isn't he doing movies like *The Outsiders* and *Rumble Fish* and *Ordinary People* and *At Close Range*? Isn't there a small part he could play in *Planes, Trains and Automobiles*? Something seems off in the world, and it isn't just that the Republicans still have control of the White House or that I have developed slight wanderlust for Adam Ant and Sting. Something is starting to feel lost that can never be found.

When my ripper wallet accidentally goes in the washing machine and my prize picture is recovered but severely damaged, I am certain a sea change is imminent.

I am twenty. It's official: I have no career and no love life. Even though I have met Ally Sheedy, Judd Nelson, Matthew Broderick, Mia Sara, Mary Stuart Masterson, Demi Moore, John Cusack, Laura Dern, Whoopi Goldberg, Woody Harrelson, Jane Fonda, Jason Patric and the entire cast of *The Lost Boys*, Sean and Chris Penn, Rob and Chad Lowe, Cher, Eric Stoltz, Jennifer Grey, Julia Roberts, Eddie Murphy, Bono, Jon Bon Jovi, and all of Ratt, Van Halen, Dokken, Cinderella, Poison, Def Leppard, and Mötley Crüe, I am jaded and depressed. Mainly because I haven't been discovered by John Hughes or run into, let alone even heard a whisper of, Michael Schoeffling, which seems like an utter impossibility considering how many others I have met so effortlessly and don't care half as much about. To make things worse, I'm not sure the whole acting thing is panning out for me, since nothing is occurring like I imagined. And though I hate to admit it, I just can't relate to John Hughes's latest flick, *The Great Outdoors*.

I join a cult. I follow an Indian guru around from Oakland to upstate New York and back again. I stay at her main ashram and do seva (selfless service) in the kitchen, chopping enough bell peppers to feed a family of four for a year. I help prepare spicy cilantro oatmeal, chai, and daal for swarms of devotees. Sometimes I help make fragrant flower garlands to place at one of the many altars on the guru's multiacre property, and sometimes I sweep the kitchen floors like a Bollywood Cinderella in a saffron and orange sari.

Always I wake up at four a.m. when we are told to, "when the ozone is best," to chant the Guru Gita and meditate just like the thousands of others here do.

In the early evenings, if we are lucky, the radiant, cocoa-skinned guru gives us daunting talks about death and enlightenment and living but for the sole purpose of dying well, about Hinduism and the complexity of its deities, about correct morals, virtues, and values arising from how subservient you can be to the guru, "for only when you can truly follow can you lead," she says. I get my priorities straight.

When I read the maxim "Truth is permanent" near the block-long laundry room where I am doing towel-folding seva, it suddenly becomes clear I have been in self-will for too long: If I am supposed to marry Michael Schoeffling, it will simply happen if and when it's meant to be. I will not have to be anything other than myself or do anything other than what is placed in my life's path. You know what ultrahot Sting says, "If you love someone set them free." A new sense of freedom follows.

In the ashram circle I meet someone. An angry, no-name actor. He wants to have sex only three times a month to conserve his Shakti so that when he dies, his kundalini will rise and shoot his soul straight out of the top of his head so he will attain enlightenment and merge with the blue pearl and oneness forevermore, like we've been taught. Fine with me; I'm a Zappa. The weirder the more familiar.

As I climb into my dormitory ladies-only bunk, I am pleased; the guru has given me focus along with my first real boyfriend.

But oddly, each day as I meditate at the grueling appointed hour in the Bade Baba Temple, back stiffened, legs folded, fingers joined, John Hughes comes to mind. The more I try to still my thoughts and let them come and go like passing clouds, the more J.H. appears.

Only, when he does, I wind up thinking about his writing process instead of becoming his next ingenue. In fact, I fixate on his process. Even if I try to push the thoughts of him out of my mind, he returns: chubby, baby-faced, bespectacled, Harvard-educated him, at his desk, a photo of someone he admires taped above his computer as he clack-clack-clacks away on the keys.

For some reason, in this ascetic environment, I take it as a sign. Something my guru is obviously trying to impart to me through her omnipresent telepathic powers. A seed is planted. I am to switch careers. I am to be a writer like my phantom mentor John Hughes. Now all I have to do is just sit back and wait for three confirmations to see if I'm right.

Back in L.A., as I return to my daily actor audition grind, even though I am vigilant in doing my predawn prostrations to the multi-armed dancing warrior, his bindied three-eyed elephant pal, and the talking blue monkey in charge of money, the psychic vision fades. Plus I just know in my heart of hearts there is an Oscar with my name on it.

One night, back in acting class, while I am sitting in the dark taking scrupulous notes in the giant black art notebook I am never without, my repetitively Oscar-thanked acting teacher interrupts himself midcritique, of two actors we are barely enduring, to announce, "Moon, you look like a writer." My ears go hot, my skin all goose pimply. It's definitely a sign.

Another evening a few months later in my parents' basement a guy comes to visit my dad. He is some kind of skateboard enthusiast and graphic artist. He's just started a magazine. On a handshake alone he offers me a writing gig, my first, a bimonthly column for *Ray Gun* magazine. I can't help but take it as sign number two.

Sign number three comes not long after, when I hear through the grapevine that Michael Schoeffling has moved somewhere back east to become a carpenter, settle down, and raise a family with his childhood sweetheart of a wife. He has given up acting. I am devastated. I am pretty sure I also hear he's Catholic.

Given the unmistakable signs confirming my guru's orders, I decide to take up writing full-time.

I am thirty-eight. I am no longer a raging Hindu, but I do spend every workday honing my internalized John Hughes–sanctioned craft, as I have for the last two decades. From magazine work to stand-up comedy, essays to short stories, screenwriting to myriad writing classes in fancy schools or someone's backyard, I am proud of every punishing, tooth-cutting step that has led me to finding my voice in ink.

Looking back on my mediocre acting career, I now lovingly view it entirely as comprehensive writing training, for one must inhabit a character's being and understand his or her motives if one wants to bring that rascal to life. As my fantasy writing mentor taught me, it also just really helps if you can give yourself some visual cues, particularly if you have a whole mess of characters running around in your story.

When I wrote my first novel, I tore an image out of a magazine for each character and posted them on the corkboard that hangs above my computer, just like ol' J.H. That way, whenever I got stuck, I'd only have to look up and imagine what mischief my character might get up to, based on a spark of a look in a stranger's pout or stony stare that inspired me. It's how I continue to work today as I type away on my next girlie romp of a book.

Nowadays I find it hilarious that my childhood obsession with Michael Schoeffling led me to gain exposure to the one man in the film industry most notorious for getting his start by obsessing, which in turn led me to a life of writing. It is now my job to obsess full-time.

Though the worn photo is long gone and I never did get to meet the oh-so-mysterious M.S. or his comedic puppet master, I am content. As a writer, I get to encounter divinity on a daily basis, worshiping at the altar of my limitless imagination. As a mom, I get to create the fun, sane atmosphere of the house for my daughter along with my husband, perfecting and putting into practice the flickers of values, life basics, and humor I observed in J.H.'s undeniably perfect films. And someday, when my baby is old enough (and if my newly remastered DVD collection can still be played on some machine in the future), I will sit down with her and watch the unequaled works I treasure and still laugh and cry at with every viewing. As my current writing teacher says, "The true artist's job is to bring people to their feet or their knees." Well, John Hughes does both.

So, as I sit here trying to write an ending to this essay about a man I never met who has single-handedly influenced my life almost as much as my own father, I find I am quite amazed. The fact that I don't even know if the information about J.H.'s work process is true doesn't even matter. All I know is that every time I sit down to write, I want my reader to feel like I did at the end of the montage in *She's Having a Baby*, when after so much turmoil you just know everything is going to be all right. I want my stories to feel like the end of *The Breakfast Club*, when the jock and the rebel and the outcast and the priss and the nerd separate, and maybe they won't all be friends when they go back to school on Monday, but they will all be different and they all shared something that can never be taken away. I want everyone to feel like I did at the end of *Sixteen Candles*, when everybody files out of the church on a deserted girl's forgotten birthday and Jake Ryan is standing there unexpectedly and you explode with cheer because Samantha got something even better than she ever could have expected.

Contributors

Steve Almond is the author of two story collections, *My Life in Heavy Metal* and *The Evil B.B. Chow*. His next book, a collection of essays, will be out in late 2007.

Julianna Baggott is the author of four novels—most recently *Which Brings Me to You* (cowritten with Steve Almond)—as well as three books of poems, including *Lizzie Borden in Love* and, forthcoming, *Compulsions of Silkworms and Bees*. She also writes novels for younger readers—the Anybodies trilogy—under the pen name N. E. Bode. Baggott's work has appeared in dozens of publications, including the *Best American Poetry* series, *Glamour*, *Ms.*, *Poetry*, and *TriQuarterly*, and has been read on National Public Radio's *Talk of the Nation*. She teaches in Florida State University's Creative Writing program and lives in Tallahassee with her husband and three children.

Lisa Borders's obsession with the 1980s was channeled into her first novel, *Cloud Cuckoo Land*, which was chosen by Pat Conroy as the winner of River City Publishing's Fred Bonnie Award and was published in 2002. She lives in Somerville, Massachusetts, where she teaches creative writing at Grub Street and works as a cytotechnologist. She recently completed her second novel, *The 51st State*.

Ryan Boudinot is the author of *The Littlest Hitler: Stories*. He lives in Seattle.

T Cooper is the author of the novels *Lipshitz Six, or Two Angry Blondes* and *Some of the Parts*. Cooper is also coeditor of a collection of original stories entitled *A Fictional History of the United States with Huge Chunks Missing*. Cooper's nonfiction work has appeared in various publications, including the *New York Times*, the *New York Times Style Magazine*, the *Believer*, and *Poets & Writers*, in addition to a handful of anthologies.

Quinn Dalton is the author of a novel, *High Strung*, and a story collection, *Bulletproof Girl*. Her stories and essays have appeared in literary magazines such as *Glimmer Train* and *One Story*, and in *New Stories from the South: The Year's Best* as well as other anthologies. She lives in Greensboro, North Carolina, with her husband and two daughters.

Emily Franklin is the author of two novels, *The Girls' Almanac* and *Liner Notes*, as well as a critically acclaimed fiction series, the Principles of Love. She edited *It's a Wonderful Lie: 26 Truths About Life in Your Twenties* and is coeditor of *Before: Short Stories About Pregnancy from Our Top Writers* and *After: Short Stories About Parenting from Our Top Writers*. Another collection, *Eight Nights: Chanukah Essays*, is forthcoming in fall 2007. Her work has appeared in the *Boston Globe* and the *Mississippi Review*, among others. She still has a crush on Jake Ryan.

Lisa Gabriele is a novelist and journalist, and her work has appeared in the *New York Times Magazine*, the *Washington Post*, *Vice* magazine, *Salon*, and *Glamour*, among other publications, and she's a regular contributor to *Nerve*. Her first novel is called *Tempting Faith DiNapoli*. Her essays and fiction have appeared in several anthologies, including *The Best American Nonrequired*

Reading 2003, *Sex and Sensibility*, and *When I Was a Loser*. She lives in Toronto.

Tod Goldberg is the author of the novels *Living Dead Girl*, a finalist for the *Los Angeles Times* Book Prize, and *Fake Liar Cheat*, as well as, most recently, the short story collection *Simplify*, winner of the Other Voices Short Story Collection Prize. His writing has appeared in the *Los Angeles Times*, *Las Vegas CityLife*, *Jewcy*, and numerous other publications. Tod Goldberg lives in La Quinta, California, and teaches creative writing at the UCLA Extension Writers' Program.

Nina de Gramont is the author of a collection of short stories, *Of Cats and Men*, and is the editor of the anthology *Choice*, forthcoming in the fall of 2007. Her novel, *Gossip of the Starlings*, will be out in August 2007. Her short stories have appeared in a variety of magazines, including *Exquisite Corpse*, the *Cream City Review*, *Nerve*, *Post Road*, and *Seventeen*.

Tara Ison's first novel, *A Child out of Alcatraz*, was a finalist for the *Los Angeles Times* Book Prize. Her new novel, *The List*, will be published in spring 2007. She is also the cowriter of the film *Don't Tell Mom the Babysitter's Dead*.

Allison Lynn is the author of the novel *Now You See It*, which won both the William Faulkner Medal from the Pirate's Alley Faulkner Society and the Chapter One Award from the Bronx Council on the Arts. She has written reviews and features for publications including the *New York Times Book Review*, the *Chicago Sun-Times*, *People*, and *In Style*. She lives in New York City and teaches creative writing at New York University.

John McNally is the author of two novels, *America's Report Card* and *The Book of Ralph*, and one story collection, *Troublemakers*. A native of southwest Chicago, he now lives in Winston-Salem, North Carolina.

Dan Pope is the author of a novel, *In the Cherry Tree*. He has published short stories in the *Iowa Review*, *McSweeney's*, *Shenandoah*, the *Gettysburg Review*, *Witness*, *Post Road*, *Crazyhorse*, and many others. He is a graduate of the Iowa Writer's Workshop.

Lewis Robinson is the author of *Officer Friendly and Other Stories*. He lives in Portland, Maine.

Ben Schrank is the author of the novels *Miracle Man* and *Consent*. He is the publisher of Razorbill, a children's book imprint at Penguin. He is at work on a third novel.

Elizabeth Searle is the author of three books and the librettist for *Tonya and Nancy: The Opera*. The opera, based on the Harding/Kerrigan scandal, premiered in the American Reperatory Theatre's space for new works in 2006, drawing coverage from the Associated Press, ESPN Hollywood, and National Public Radio. Searle's books are *My Body to You*, winner of the Iowa Short Fiction Award; *A Four-Sided Bed*, a novel nominated for an American Library Association book award; and *Celebrities in Disgrace*, forthcoming as a short film. She teaches in the Stonecoast MFA Program.

Mary Sullivan is the author of *Ship Sooner* and *Stay*. She has received a Massachusetts Cultural Council grant, a Rona Jaffe Foundation Writers' Award, and a St. Botolph Club Foundation Award. She lives in Cambridge, Massachusetts, with her husband and their two daughters.

Rebecca Wolff was born in New York City in 1967. Right around 1981 she hit Stuyvesant High School, where she took great pains with her hair color. Her books of poems are *Manderley* and *Figment*. She is the founding editor of the magazine *Fence* and Fence Books. She lives in the Hudson Valley with her husband, the novelist Ira Sher, and their two children.

Moon Unit Zappa is a writer, filmmaker, wife, and mom who would happily come out of acting seclusion to make out with Michael Schoeffling under the keen and watchful writing/direction of John Hughes.

Printed in Great Britain
by Amazon

11603835R00130